THE TECHNIQUES OF

PAINTING MINIATURES

THE TECHNIQUES OF PAINTING MINIATURES

SUE BURTON

B. T. BATSFORD • LONDON

First published 1995

Design and typeset by
David Quay
Sutchinda Thompson

and printed in
Hong Kong

Published by
B. T. Batsford Ltd,
4 Fitzhardinge Street,
London W1H 0AH

A catalogue record for
this book is available
from the British Library

ISBN 0 7134 7459 9

Half title page plate:
Gillie
Heather O. Catchpole
Watercolour on
Ivorine. *9 x 7 cm (3 1/2 x
2 3/4 in)*

Title page plate:
Four O'Clock
Elaine Fellows
Watercolour on
vellum. *5 x 6.25 cm
(2 x 2 1/2 in)*

ACKNOWLEDGEMENTS

I WOULD LIKE TO THANK all the people who have helped me put this book together.

First the artists who agreed to show me exactly how they paint and gave away professional secrets to help others learn about their art. Making the choice of who to ask was extremely difficult. I wanted to cover every aspect without being repetitious and to stretch the different approaches to the maximum, whilst keeping within the boundaries of exemplary miniatures. On the other hand I could not include all the wonderful artists there are in this field.

Then there are the 'proofreaders', friends of many talents, who have had the double duty of encouraging and putting up with me throughout.

Finally all the people around the world who kept me up to date with information, sometimes sending quite large packages with generous enthusiasm and no complaints.

You all know who you are.
Thank You.

Llewellyn Alexander Gallery

Historical Miniatures

The Llewellyn Alexander Fine Art Gallery, London, kindly facilitated the loan of transparencies of the older miniatures from the Bridgeman Museum Library.

Photographs of Contemporary Paintings

by David Titchener ABIPP AMPA

Contents

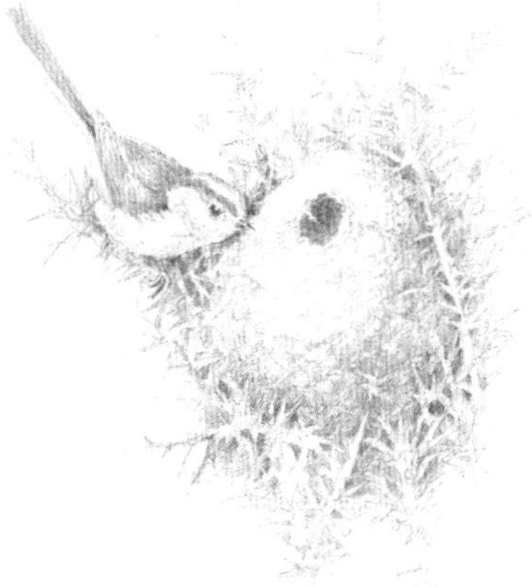

Nemesias
watercolour on ivory
by Suzanne Lucas FLS PRMS

Introduction

This is a book compiled from fifteen years of listening to artists who paint miniatures. I have unashamedly eavesdropped, picked their brains and derived immense pleasure from looking at their work. They are a most generous group of people and share their knowledge unreservedly. If you discover another beautiful new aspect of painting through this book, it is the artists who should be thanked for giving their time and expertise. This is their book, I only put it together.

Twenty years ago I knew next to nothing about miniature art. My art history textbook at school had Nicholas Hilliard's famous miniature of the young man among the roses on the cover. Considering it was deemed to contain enough information to enable us to learn about the history of all fields of English art, I find that a little ironic now.

The opinion has been voiced that miniature painting is more about craftsmanship. If that means the miniaturist has more technique to master, before being able to add the inspiration as well, I agree. Good drawing is essential and this comes from good observation. One mistake and hours of work can be ruined. The concentration that goes into the work shines out from a good miniature and every detail is noticed. It is a disciplined and painstaking process. Miniatures can never be rushed and people do not tend to 'get quicker at it', quite the reverse; often the more they learn, the slower they become. It is 'fine art'.

I would like to quote Suzanne Lucas, President of the Royal Society of Miniature Painters, Sculptors and Gravers:

> *'Miniature art demands self-discipline, for where large paintings give some latitude in composition, miniatures are unforgiving of the least mistake: a tolerance of even a millimetre is hardly permitted. The physical control to keep absolutely still while at work, because an unrelated movement might spoil the sensitive stroke, is very tiring as one realizes when painting a miniature where the brush strokes may run to half a million in number and each must be of a precise depth and colour, consistency and application.'*

Ego autem ſicut oliua fructifera in
domo Dei ſperaui in miſericordia Dei
in eternum, & in ſeculum ſeculi.
Confitebor tibi in ſeculum quia feciſti
& expectabo nomen tuum quoniam bonū eſt
in conſpectu ſanctorum tuorum Gloria
patri Sicut erat.
Dixit
inſipiēs
in corde
ſuo nō
eſt Deꝰ
Cor=
rupti ſūt

Henry VIII and his Fool, Will Somers
Reproduced by kind permission of The British Library, London.

Actual size

What is a Miniature Painting?

The word 'miniature' did not originally refer to size. One of the weightier volumes of the Oxford English Dictionary states: 'The small size characteristic of paintings in miniature has lead to a pseudo-etymological association of the word with the Latin Min – expressing smallness *(in minor = less and minimus = least, minuere = to diminish)* which has probably affected the development of the transferred and figurative senses.' Whichever dictionary you consult, you immediately find information about illuminated manuscripts and 'miniature' seems to be derived from *minium* (red lead). This pigment was used for the ornamental borders, headings and wonderfully ornate initial letters in manuscripts on vellum. It is a little difficult to stretch the association with sumptuous illuminated manuscripts in gold leaf and vermilion to some of the modern uses of the word 'miniature'. But it shows that we should not become too hide-bound; if the art of miniature painting is not to die, it must evolve. At the same time, the basics of what constitutes a miniature painting should not be lost either.

Modern English miniature painting certainly has its roots in the illuminations of the fifteenth and sixteenth centuries. The more accurate term may be 'limnings' or, as Horace Walpole described them, 'paintings in little' but in this book they will be referred to as miniatures. Henry VIII and his wives sat for some of the earliest miniature portraits, by then elevated into an art form in its own right. These paintings were used as photographs would be today: they identified and authenticated. They were small, easily transportable and could be hidden in closed lockets, which meant they could also be secret and intimate. For historians, these portraits must reveal a most intriguing private side of life. There were also 'cabinet' miniatures that could be free standing or could hang on a wall. One of these by Isaac Oliver, painted *c.*1605-10, is on vellum and includes a large proportion of landscape. It measures just over 17.5 x 22.5 centimetres (7 x 9 inches).

Left
Ann of Cleves, by Hans Holbein. Diameter 4.6 cm (1 3/4 inch).

Since this is not to be a book on the history of miniatures, I will not dwell on the subject but it is interesting to chart the most important changes. The earliest surviving English paintings were done by artists to the Tudor court. Lucas Hornebolte painted Henry VIII in 1525-56. Hans Holbein was sent by the King to do a likeness of Anne of Cleves in 1539 and painted many other marvellous miniature portraits. Levina Teerlinc arrived on the scene in 1546 and may have instructed Nicholas Hilliard (1547-1619). Born in Exeter, the son of a goldsmith, Hilliard was the first great English miniaturist. Due to religious uprisings in Exeter at that time, his father, who played a leading part in this disturbance, placed him with the Bodley household. The son, Thomas, was founder of the Bodleian Library. This association would probably have exposed Hilliard to illuminated manuscripts at about nine years old. The Bodley family were forced to flee the country when Queen Mary came to power and so the young Hilliard travelled to Europe. He produced three (known) miniature portraits when he was about thirteen years old. In about 1660 he was persuaded to compose the 'Treatise concerning the Art of Limning', the first time any information on how to paint miniatures had been documented.

Hilliard painted very clear, defined portraits with few shadows. The paints he used were mainly opaque, with stippling and modelling in transparent colours to show the features. The paintings were highly decorative and his background in jewellery led him to lay transparent colour, bound by resin, over burnished silver to give reality to the gems worn by his sitters. In one portrait of Elizabeth I he has actually set a tiny table-cut diamond in the centre of the orb she is holding. He 'treacled' white on to the painting to show the exquisitely detailed lace; under a strong magnifying glass (and you need one to

Portrait of a Young Man, by Nicholas Hilliard. Reproduced by kind permission of the Victoria and Albert Museum, London. *Actual size*

Right
The Gresley Jewel, with portraits of Sir Thomas Gresley and his bride Catherine Walsingham, by Nicholas Hilliard. Reproduced by kind permission of the Bridgeman Art Library.
Actual size

appreciate it) it looks almost three-dimensional. These paintings were executed on fine vellum and are set into extremely elaborate, engraved and bejewelled frames.

Isaac Oliver (1551-1617) was, to my mind, the first specialist miniature painter to produce sensitive and life-like portraits. He used more stippling in the modelling of the features to give a soft roundness to cheeks and other areas, making them less flat and linear. The clothes and draperies were fuller and the shadows deeper. He took the art a step away from that of the illuminator and launched the long tradition of portrait miniatures which continued almost unabated until the advent of photography, although there are still portrait artists today producing marvellous work.

The early painters used mostly natural pigments that they ground themselves and bound with gum arabic. Whites were made from white lead (mixed with whitening), chalk, gypsum, eggshells or oyster shells. White lead mixed with a little red lead (*minium*) seems to have been used for the 'carnation', the word used for skin tones. Hilliard, we are told, used velvet black, which was obtained from burning ivory, but he also used cherry stones, peach stones and charcoal made from willow. Then there was lamp black which was soot obtained from 'burning with an insufficient supply of air'. When we start to investigate the colours, the variations are endless and the sources of pigments worldwide. It is a fascinating subject but must have been a tedious business to go through before a painting was even begun. There is a portrait executed in 'pigment bound with oil' dated around 1650. Samuel Cooper (1609-1672), who retained his popularity despite the Civil War, gives us a wonderful example of work in progress in his unfinished portrait of Oliver Cromwell, (see page 15) painted on vellum.

Vellum pasted on to card was the most commonly

Left
Countess Frances Howard,
by Isaac Oliver.
Reproduced by kind permission of the Bridgeman Art Library.
Actual size

Right
Oliver Cromwell, *(unfinished)*
by Samuel Cooper.
Reproduced by kind permission of the Bridgeman Art Library.
Actual size

used base, or ground, until the early 1700s. An Italian artist, Rosalba Carriera, is first credited with experimenting with ivory and by the 1720s ivory was being widely used in England. Bernard Lens (1682-1740) was among the first to use this new base, although he still worked in mainly opaque colours. Gradually the use of transparent colour was perfected. It was floated on to the surface to build up the layers of clear colour that utilized the translucence of ivory so beautifully, especially for skin tones. Richard Cosway (1742-1821) discovered its full potential. The ivory bases became thinner by the end of the century. Eventually smooth surfaced paper or card could be used as an alternative until Ivorine came into use in the 1920s and was added to the list of possible supports. Today ivory, due to considerations of cost and conservation, has almost disappeared but a miniature can be painted on as wide a variety of bases as larger works provided the surface is smooth enough to facilitate the detail and delicacy of the brush strokes.

Towards the end of the nineteenth century ivory was sometimes coated with light-sensitive chemicals and paintings were then executed over the faint photographic images obtained. This was the ultimate combination of photograph and miniature, allowing more affordable portraits but naturally upsetting the purist. In the opinion of museums, few true miniatures have been painted since the arrival of photography so it seems strange that the Royal Society of Miniature Painters, Sculptors and Gravers, still extremely active, was started in 1895.

Detail showing the intricacy of the work on the hair and veil of **Countess Frances Howard**, by Isaac Oliver.

In the last hundred years subject matter has changed enormously. Whilst landscape was used in some past miniatures it tended to be as a background to the figures. Now, any subject — be it still-life, botanical, landscape, animals, architectural or anything anyone may be inspired to paint — can be classed as a miniature. So what are the elements that define a modern miniature and at what scale does a 'small painting' become a 'painting in little'?

There is no hard and fast rule of measurement. The easiest definition is that a head (as in a human portrait) should not exceed 5 centimetres (2 inches). Fine work, stippling and minute attention to detail are still, as they have always been, part of the art. Subjects, of any sort, should be less than life size. A larger than life size study of a tiny flower could be very small but it would not be a miniature. A scale rule as a set ratio of reduction for every subject does not really work. An elephant would still be too big to fit in a miniature if the same ratio of reduction was applied to it as, for instance, to a forget-me-not. A painting that is tiny, but that would not stand the test of being enlarged without revealing its faults is not acceptable either. One loose definition is a painting that can be held in the hand. It must stand close inspection. It must not look as though it is part of a larger painting and therefore unsatisfactory because something is missing. It should give the feeling of being complete and whole in composition; of belonging only to itself. When a miniature painting is good, the viewer is drawn into a concentrated little world that is breathtaking in its execution.

The following chapters should make the definition clearer as some of the leading miniature artists generously share their knowledge and illustrate their different techniques. Perhaps it is only through the example of the best exponents of the art of modern miniature painting that anything approaching a definition can be arrived at.

FOUR HUNDRED YEARS OF MINIATURE ART

Thomas, 2nd Earl of Arundel, by Isaac Oliver, **1595**. *Actual size*

Simon, by Dorothy Bushell, **1995**. *Actual size*

TECHNIQUES

BASES Miniatures can be originated on any surface that facilitates the production of fine detail. Artists owe a responsibility to the purchasers of their work to choose something which will not deteriorate but apart from that it is a matter of personal choice. It is advisable to obtain fine quality materials from reliable sources as this leads to less frustration in the end. Miniaturists, by the very nature of what they do, tend to be fastidious with an eye for detail. Bases that are not clean are going to cause problems. Vellum that is not of the finest quality may have a flaw in the surface which will interfere with the work. Paper and board should be acid free because acid reacts with damp in the atmosphere and causes the work to yellow and deteriorate.

I have included ivory because it is so intrinsically linked with miniature technique, although it may upset some people. I do not wish to encourage anyone to use illegally obtained ivory. It is intolerable that such a wonderful animal as an elephant should have to die to produce a miniature, but what do you do with the old ivory that is still around? I know the ends of the tusks of working elephants are sawn off and capped to stop them splitting and I suppose some elephants are culled for good animal husbandry reasons. Can you be sure, however, that that is the way any piece of ivory came to be in your hand? It is a very emotive subject which each artist must make up his or her own mind about.

Ivory, mother of pearl and similar substances

These substances are used in such a way that the intrinsic translucence and shine of the base material becomes part of the painting. Apparently there is a supply of mammoth tusk becoming available which may take the place of elephant ivory. Whatever the base it must be scrupulously clean to start with. The surface can be slightly roughened with pumice powder or any other gentle abrasive, but only to give it a slight 'tooth' to hold the paint. It should not cause any obvious lines to appear. To take most advantage of these beautiful surfaces, clear, transparent watercolour

Facing page
A selection of brushes, surfaces and frames. The box opens out to reveal pans of water-colour and a palette for mixing.

is 'floated' on in several layers, allowing each layer to dry before applying the next; the more layers the more intense the colour. (See excellent example of this on page 8.)

Some artists cut the base to size before they start; to have taken weeks to complete a portrait and then split the base when cutting it into shape (particularly difficult with curves) would be disastrous. Ivory is very much like a fingernail which can split along the length if not cut sympathetically with the grain. If you do find it necessary, cut up towards the centre on each side in short little cuts, just as you would a fingernail.

Ivorine Ivorine is a plastic (cellulose nitrate) substitute for ivory. It is made from materials similar to those used for table tennis balls. There has been a lot of debate recently about its lasting qualities as all plastics degrade eventually. We know that Ivorine paintings done in the 1930s are still in good condition today if they have been cared for correctly. This means not exposing them excessively to the three main things that cause degeneration: Ultra-Violet light, heat and oxygen. This is true of most paintings and as long as you treat the work with due care and don't use fugitive paints there should not be any great problem.

The surface should be perfectly clean before you apply any paint. Fingermarks are greasy and will make the colour 'shrink'. Spit from someone talking over the work lifts the paint, as can other dirt. It is very sad to see a painting peeling after hours of work, just because the artist did not make sure the surface was clean in the first place. If the Ivorine has been obtained from a reliable source and stored carefully it may not need anything doing to it. Otherwise there are various methods of cleaning and degreasing it. Many artists use detergents and some even use brass cleaners, but that seems a little excessive if the Ivorine has not been abused. Whatever method you use, you have to be sure that all traces of the cleaner are removed as well or the paint could become grainy or 'chalky' or even change colour. The two most popular methods are either talcum

Girl with Violin by Michael Coe; watercolour on Ivorine. *Actual size.* Michael uses tiny amounts of paint applied in short brushstrokes using a size 000 sable brush. He is meticulous about cleanliness throughout the six to eight weeks it takes him to complete a painting.

powder rubbed over the surface and then removed with a tissue or cottonwool, or a putty eraser rubbed over the surface. Again, great care should be taken to eliminate any residue. A slightly more emphatic way of removing grease is to use flour paper which is the equivalent of very fine sandpaper. Pumice powder is another fairly tough cleaning agent. Some paints will stain Ivorine if left too long but as a rule any mistakes can be washed out or corrected quite easily. I have even been shown an example of Ivorine, painted over in oils several years before, that, when the paint was removed with a fibre-glass eraser, was perfectly capable of being used again! It is a very forgiving surface in that respect.

Fine hot-pressed paper

Fine hot-pressed paper is always reliable. The choice is up to the artist as to how 'moppy' or 'filled' a surface they prefer, depending on whether they want to achieve a wash or rely mainly on stippling and cross hatching. One or two artists even use a paper with a slight texture to it, but it is difficult to maintain fine detail on a rough surface. One advantage for the miniaturist is that one sheet of expensive best quality paper can be cut up and used for several paintings.

Vellum

Vellum, whilst perhaps not as controversial to some people as ivory, can still give vegetarians a problem of conscience. The story that the best vellum is aborted calfskin is true to some extent, if you take the finest to mean the most hairless. However, nobody is going to deliberately abort calves to produce vellum — it wouldn't be cost effective! The suppliers point out that the skins they use are 'waste products' and no animal is killed simply to produce parchment or vellum.

There is a choice as to the grade of vellum you decide to use. There are calfskin and goatskin vellums; parchment (sheepskin or goatskin) is different, being thicker with markings that could be inconvenient for miniature artwork. Calfskin manuscript vellum has a slightly rough surface, which may need smoothing with pumice. Classic calfskin vellum is cream coloured and is used for calligraphy and bookbinding. Kelmscott vellum is a manuscript vellum that has had the surface filled to make it thick and smooth. There is a hair side and a flesh side to all vellum, the flesh side is the smoothest but may have marks from veins. Since miniaturists use such a small surface area, it is possible to avoid blemishes. As with most materials the best quality is usually the most expensive and the 'finest' to work on. If you are experimenting for the first time, obtain offcuts to get the feel of the different surfaces.

Stick the vellum down on to acid-free card to make it easier to handle and to stop it cockling. Alternatively, it can be taped at the corners to keep it from moving too much. Even a change in the weather can make vellum warp if it is not held down. Small pieces can be flattened under a heavy book, prior to painting. A precut 'working mount' placed over the piece of vellum and taped in place will stop you resting your hand on it whilst painting. Pumice powder will remove grease and is mildly abrasive. Ox-gall rubbed over the surface, evenly but lightly, provides a good 'key' and gets rid of grease.

Vellum is an absorbent surface that gives wonderful crisp detail. Mistakes can be very carefully scratched out with a scalpel, as can highlights.

Hardboard or copper

Hardboard (smooth side up) or copper is the usual base for oil paints although Ivorine (prepared as already mentioned) is often used as well. It is advisable to prime hardboard and copper to seal the surface and to create the smooth base desirable for fine work. Gesso primer or a white oil paint is suitable. To make sure there are no

Landscape by Alois Majzlik showing oil on a copper base. *Actual size*

brushmarks from applying the primer, it is advisable to rub the surface down with fine sandpaper or even flour paper when dry and to use two or more thin coats if necessary. Copper should also be sealed on the back surface as it can corrode. If the surface of the copper is required to shine through, the paint can be removed where required (it scrapes off quite easily). Alternatively, clear varnish can be used instead of white primer as a glaze underneath, to give the paint a surface to adhere to. Varnish must be applied to the finished oil painting, following the same rules as for larger work. Spray varnish covers evenly, but if ordinary varnish is gently warmed before use it should be possible to apply without brushmarks.

Fabrics Fabrics such as silk, handkerchief linen or cotton and very fine canvases have been used for tiny oil paintings but this usually means stretching them over a purpose-built stretcher made to size by the artist. Alternatively, card can support the material without stretchers. The material chosen should be stuck down firmly and then primed. These bases should be treated in the same way as larger canvases — but delicately. It is very difficult to control the paint on untreated silk as it tends to bleed into the material if there is nothing to stop it. This produces wonderful effects for the larger scale painter to take advantage of but is highly risky within the confines of a miniature. There are specific mediums that stop the paint spreading. Acrylic, oil or watercolours require different mediums but some are interchangeable. A very attractive result can be produced when a painting has been assembled exactly as a larger work would be but scaled down throughout.

PAINTS These should always be best artists' quality and as lightfast as possible. Only very small amounts are used, so you may as well treat yourself to 'the best' from the beginning. The grainy texture of some students' colours could make the paint feel chalky and impair the flow off the brush. Miniaturists tend to use more intense colour in tiny amounts; muddy or indefinite colours do not usually work so well for miniature technique.

Some of the colours listed by the individual artists may soon not be available because of newly introduced EEC safety regulations. Vermilion, which appears in many of the portrait painters' palettes, is one of them. It can be replaced by Cadmium Red Light, and there are synthetic alternatives.

Pan and tube watercolour paints.

Watercolours Watercolours have advantages and disadvantages as to the packaging. Pans (or half-pans) of watercolours wear out brushes faster than paint from tubes, which is a consideration when you are using expensive best quality sable brushes. Tubes can dry out, especially if they are colours you don't use very often and you can waste paint by squeezing out too much at a time. It is an individual choice; some artists use both pans and tubes. The artists who prefer tubes say the paint stays cleaner and fresher. Some squeeze tube paints into empty half-pans. Others cut the bottoms off the tubes and use the dried up paint from the 'wrong' end! Several artists I spoke to had had their tubes of paints for ten to twenty years. One advised losing the top to the tube as soon as possible as 'fresh' paint was too sticky. Where one artist will swear by a certain make of paint, another will find it too plastic in texture. The colours, although called the same name, may be considerably brighter or deeper. I think miniaturists feel the texture of their paint as it goes on, more than most artists. It is a matter of looking at what appeals to you in other people's work and then experimenting with different makes of paint yourself. Even different pigments give different textures.

Oil paints Oil paints are covered by the same ground rules as watercolours. Always endeavour to use the best quality for colourfastness and clarity of colour. Thinning agents are important; where the watercolourist can use water from the tap, the oil painter has to find a way of transferring very small amounts of paint on to the 'canvas' with the aid of a medium. Paint straight from the tube can be extremely thick for miniature work. Linseed oil was not popular with most of the artists I spoke to, the consensus of opinion was that it made the paint too tacky. Pure turpentine seemed to be the choice. There are products such as artists' painting media which may be useful to enhance the flow where glazes of clear colour are built up.

Pastels Pastels are extremely difficult to use for fine work. The softer ones can be sharpened with a pencil sharpener and the dust applied with a tortillon or screw of paper. I have seen it done well but pastels and miniature work are almost mutually exclusive. I would not want to put anyone off trying but they will be giving themselves a hard task.

Acrylics Acrylics also come packed in fairly large tubes, which are going to last a long time if you only paint miniatures. Once again buy best quality artists' colours. Not only will they help you to produce the best work, they keep longer. There is a multitude of products to mix with acrylics; some to make them dry faster, some to retard them and others to improve the flow. Which you choose depends very much on the way you wish to handle the paint. Acrylics can be used as watercolours or in the same manner as oils. They are amongst the most versatile media available and have the advantage that the brushes can be washed in water.

Square Riggers, by Cdr. G. Hunt. Acrylic on Board. 9.2 x 15 cm (3½ x 6 in)

BRUSHES Almost every miniaturist is primarily concerned with the point of the brush, especially the watercolourist. Best Kolinsky sable is usually the first choice for any type of paint. If the supplier will allow you (you could go somewhere else if he won't), ask for a glass of clean water and dip the brush into it and flick the water out. If the point splits try another. You can also roll the wet sable very gently on the back of your hand to see if the point has any hairs sticking out. The length of the bristle varies according to which 'series' or type you use; this is a personal preference, as is the handle, which varies slightly in length and weight. I know some artists who chop the handle down to shorten it by as much as a third. Those sold as miniaturists' brushes are usually shorter bristled for more control, but it is not obligatory to work that way. Do not be led into believing any nonsense about one or two hairs either; a good reservoir of paint is vital and that can only be held in a brush with a lot of hairs. Some artists use up to size 4 (English size) as long as it has a good point, although 000, 00, 0 and 1 are more usual. Oil painters use small bristle brushes of various shapes as well as sable.

I have yet to hear of a palette knife miniaturist (using a scalpel blade perhaps?) but you never know. A needle comes in handy for scratching out.

John, by Elizabeth Meek.
A wonderful example of fine brush strokes where the paint is applied in continuous lines the way the hair would grow. 11.9 x 7.7 cm (4½ x 3 in)

APPLYING THE PAINT

I am not trying to teach people how to paint in this book; colour mixing and the basics of composition and perspective can be practised and read about elsewhere. The object is to assist with techniques where miniatures differ from larger works.

Stippling and hatching certainly help and are a good discipline to practise if you want to produce crisp, clear paintings. Few miniaturists are interested in washes, except perhaps for skies. A layer of paint can be 'floated' on with watercolour, left to harden by drying and then another layer placed over the first to increase the intensity of clear, transparent colour. Very thin glazes can be used with oils. Shadows are best built up this way. Remember white oil paint is opaque and does not need such a build up so can be used to give more texture to surfaces. This all takes practice and confidence and I am referring to very small areas. If watercolours are overworked, paint will be lifted off rather than put on, especially on surfaces like Ivorine; this can also be true of stippling. Patience is the key word — very small quantities of paint should be applied at a time and allowed to harden before being worked over again, and again, if necessary. So often beginners get decidedly 'woolly' results and it seems to be largely due to trying to go on too fast or getting too thick a build up of paint. Do not allow yourself to be rushed by anything or anybody.

Right
Hatching

Far right
Stippling

As shown by Christine Hart-Davies and described in her method of working (see pp. 98-101).

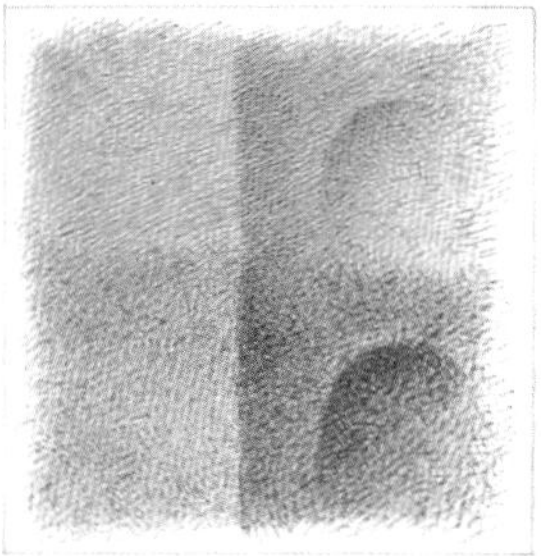

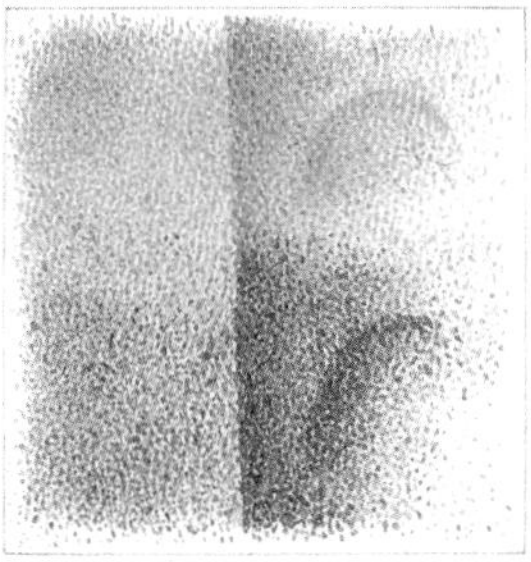

Hints and tips

Keep everything clean. Always cover your work with a 'box' larger than the painting if you leave it before completion or drying, even if it is only to answer the telephone. Some miniatures take weeks to finish and this simple precaution may save the heartbreak of picking bits of fluff off the surface. The box can be clear plastic so that other people know what is under it or you could use a heavier glass kitchen dish if there are animals around. Put the painting away if left for any length of time and check it with a magnifying glass each time you resume painting.

Painting miniatures is an absorbing pastime that taxes concentration, eyesight and neck, arm and back muscles to a degree that may not be appreciated unless you have tried it. Whether you paint flat on a table or upright on a drawing board is a matter of personal preference. Try to arrange youı workspace so that the table is high enough for you not to have to bend over for hours on end. One artist has a wooden box on top of a normal table in order to raise the work; quite a number are in favour of secretarial chairs or stools with no backs and a knee rest. Not many artists can work for hours at a stretch without a break and it is a good idea to order your day so that this does not happen. Frequent coffee breaks at set times and routines that allow time out or at least a change of activity are advisable for you as well as letting the paint dry for the next layer. It is up to the individual but I have known people taking up miniature painting to become 'hooked' — they cannot stop and are at it until three o'clock in the morning! This is all right for a while but some artists develop serious muscular problems from bad sitting habits and backstrain. It is better to think of sensible ways of painting from the start so that you do not run the risk of being forced to stop later on.

Good eyesight is a bonus but a great number of miniaturists wear glasses and many use magnifying glasses to check their work. Spectacles can be made especially to facilitate close work — an optician will advise you. The distance between your work and your eye can be measured and purposely prescribed glasses (with a tolerance of a couple of inches) made up for you. Headbands with magnification lenses built in are available, as are magnifying lenses on stands with daylight bulbs built around the underside. A good miniature painting should not need to be looked at through a magnifying glass, but if you want to see how the work has been achieved a glass will show all the minute brush strokes of carefully placed colours that go to make up the whole.

It is difficult to paint miniatures out of doors. Instead, sketches can be made in the time-honoured way and photographic records taken. Then it is very much easier and more practical to go back to the studio.

Setting and safeguarding your work, as advised by Sheila Sanford *(see pp. 74-77)*.

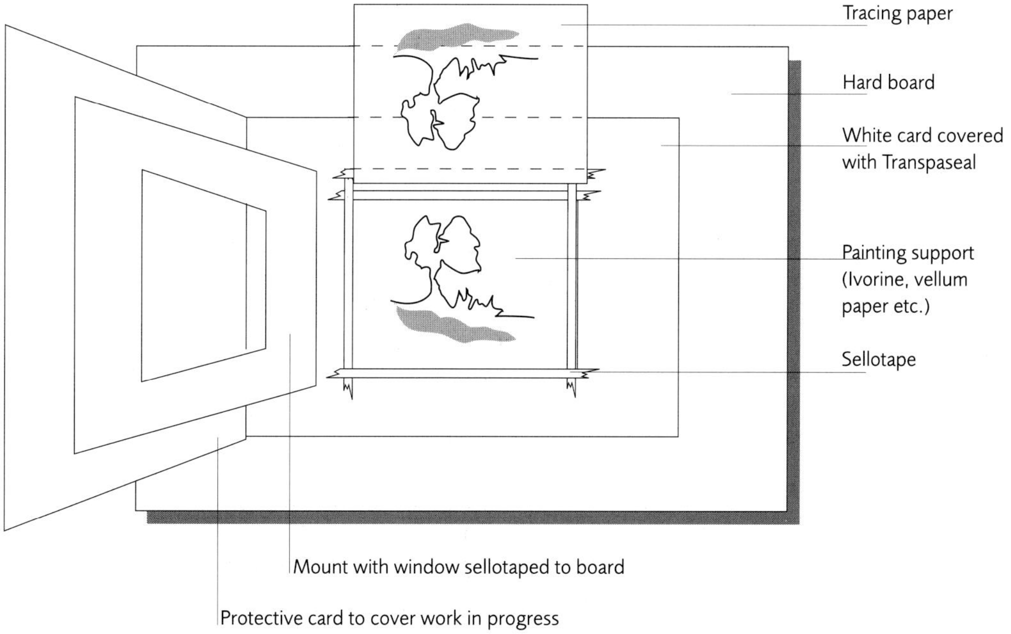

FRAMING

This is an emotive subject and you will never please everybody whatever you do. First you have to consider the reason for framing. It protects the painting and facilitates hanging or display of some sort. Watercolour paint should never touch the glass used to protect it, hence the need for a mount or convex glass. If there is no air space, condensation can cause irreparable damage and mould will grow; pastels and watercolours can become stuck to the glass. Oils and paintings in acrylics (where the acrylics have been applied in the same manner) do not need the protection of glass but they must be varnished. Glass may be used if wished, as long as it is kept from touching the painting. All mounts and boards should be acid free, for conservation.

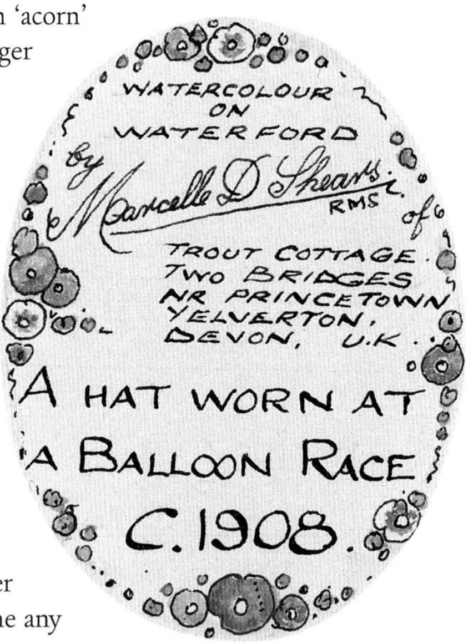

Right
The front and back views of **A Hat Worn at the Balloon Race**, by Marcelle Shears. Marcelle is fastidious about cleanliness and takes as much care with the back of the frame as she does with the actual painting.

The traditional gold coloured (or gold plated) frame, usually oval with convex glass, is still used as much as anything, especially for portraits, as is the acorn frame. This, a rectangular black surround to an oval, has an 'acorn' holding the ring at the top. Mouldings used for larger works can equally well be used for miniatures. Mounts are cut in the same way, to keep the painting from touching the glass. The only point to make here is that they have to be cut as carefully as the painting has been painted. Any error will be very noticeable as the eye goes to every detail on a miniature. Some miniatures look very attractive framed 'large', with a wide area of mount surround. It can make more of a feature of them when they are hung on a wall. One thing I find upsetting is when the frame is 'distressed' to make it look older: the blotches look gross next to a miniature because they are so out of scale and so obviously splattered on. This disturbing problem of scale can also be true of other details on ornate frames; it is always wrong to frame any

painting so that you notice the frame before you see the picture. For instance, if you use a wide, brassy frame on a muted, delicate watercolour you have to force your eye to look at the painting. A frame should always complement the painting, without intruding into it. If in doubt choose the plainest.

Left
Chilton Foliat,
by Robert Hughes
6 x 7.5 cm ($2\frac{1}{2}$ x 3 in)

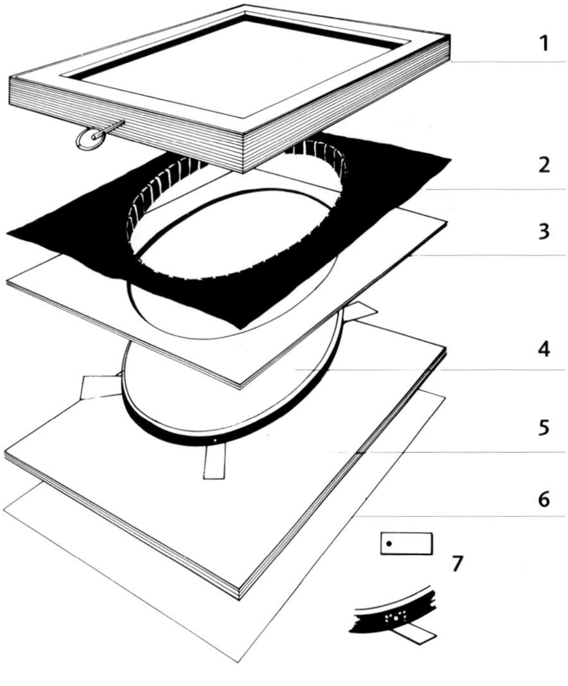

Right
Framing as practised by Sydney Shorthouse. He sets the traditional oval off against a sympathetic colour velvet and secures this within a larger rectangular frame for displaying on a wall.

1 Frame made up from a wooden moulding with ring at the top for hanging.
2 Velvet covering to be stuck to the board below, eventually forming a surround for the painting in a metal oval frame. Cut oval smaller than required finished size and snip the edge to facilitate folding under and gluing, giving a neat finished edge, tight to the frame.
3 Mount board with exact size oval cut in it to take the metal oval frame (**4**). Use this frame as template.
4 Gold or metal oval complete with glass as obtained from the supplier. Cut strips of aluminium and bend at right angles to slip in between gold frame and oval backing board. These are then held when the pins are put in place (see **7**) and are used to secure the oval to the velvet-covered board.
5 Backing board of sufficient thickness to keep everything in place when all assembled.
6 Backing of paper or material to finish the reverse off neatly.
7 Strips of aluminium used to secure the oval.

Jane
watercolour on Ivorine
by Dorothy Bushell

Actual size

Portraits

Dorothy Bushell

Watercolour on Ivorine

Dorothy Bushell is one of the best portrait artists working today, combining technical excellence with a soft and human result. She works from photographs that she has taken herself; she used to make sketches as well but rarely does so now. By photographing many different views of the sitter she can make up a composite portrait. If she has any difficulty with the proportions of the features, she refers to all the photographs she has taken to make corrections. Although she says she is no photographer, she obviously knows what she is looking for. A studio photographic portrait, using professional lighting, does not suit her at all and she tries to avoid commissions that entail working from this type of material. Instead she prefers to meet her sitters wherever possible but she will work from photographs supplied by the client if there is no alternative.

Dorothy only works in daylight, sitting at a table set at a right angle to a large window. Since she is right-handed, the light comes from her left. Artificial light seems to reflect back at her disturbingly and she avoids using it. She uses a head magnifier, worn like a visor, while she is painting, leaving her hands free.

First the surface of the Ivorine must be perfectly clean. To achieve this, she rubs it over with pumice powder, using cottonwool. It must then be thoroughly dusted off with fresh cottonwool. She then tapes a piece of fairly strong white paper securely to a board. This has four slots cut in it at angles to fit the corners of the piece of Ivorine. The square of Ivorine is then slotted in at the corners, which hold it firm for painting. The paper has to be white as Ivorine will allow whatever is underneath to show through. If the base has already been cut into an oval, she uses double-sided tape on the back to keep it firm. The board can be turned or picked up at will without touching the painting.

If the frame is to be the traditional oval, it is measured and the outline drawn on the Ivorine to make sure the painting stays within bounds. Dorothy never uses pencil

Paints
(usual palette)
Winsor & Newton artists' quality watercolours in half-pans:
Yellow Ochre
Chrome Yellow
Burnt Sienna
Vermilion (usually mixed with a touch of yellow to give a glow to the skin).
She also uses the slightest touch of green sometimes.

Base
Ivorine
(Will use old ivory if the purchaser requests it, cut to size and shaped before painting begins, otherwise treated the same as Ivorine.)

Brushes
Winsor & Newton, best sable, series 7, size 2.

Other materials
Pumice powder
Cottonwool
Masking tape
Water to dilute
Magnifying lens, worn on a band round the head, leaving the hands free.

1
The image is achieved by first drawing and then building up the colours in very pale neutral shades of the finished tones.

2
The background and different areas of the face are gradually built up keeping an overall balance of strength of colour.

3
Each subsequent layer of paint holds better over the preceding ones, allowing more and more precision with the stippled modelling of the features.

The finished painting enlarged to show the brush strokes and detail.

as she has found through experience that the graphite can smudge. To mark lines on the base she paints them on with a brush. The image is achieved by drawing in the rough outline of the head freehand straight on to the Ivorine, using a soft, very pale, neutral-colour paint. She measures off from the centre of the eye, comparing the width with the length of the face, but otherwise she judges by eye. To correct a mistake, she moistens a clean brush on her tongue and removes the paint stroke by stroke — an old photographic retouching trick.

Next she starts to build up the face. Once the features, contours and modelling have been established, she focuses on the clothes. She works on the background before returning to the face in more detail. In this way, every aspect of the painting is kept in balance. She lets the first layer of colour shine through to the finished layers to give lustre to the hair, for example. The contours of the face are modelled by stippling rather than using any washes. Dorothy sometimes turns the painting upside down to compare it with the photographs, making sure at every stage that the proportions are correct.

One point she advises strongly is not to try to achieve an immediate depth of colour too quickly. She has washed a painting off before now because she feels it has become too strong too quickly. A straightforward, simple miniature, where the likeness comes quickly and everything goes well, could take her about thirty hours. Sometimes the dress alone can take three to four days.

She stops when she feels it 'has arrived.' Then the painting is put away for a while, a week at least, and not looked at at all. When she takes it out again, if something strikes her eye immediately she knows it is wrong.

Dorothy always frames her portraits in traditional oval frames, usually gold. A piece of white paper, cut the same size, is placed behind the Ivorine in the frame. This is left loose as it should not move if it has been cut accurately. It provides a clear white to shine through the Ivorine making the most of its translucent quality.

Gillie Hoyte Byrom
Fired Vitrified Enamel on Copper

Sir John Harvey-Jones, portrait in enamels by Gillie Hoyte-Byrom.
Actual size
One of the advantages of enamels is that after the final firing the painting is safe; the colours will never alter unless subjected to heat at 850° centigrade.

Enamelling is really a subject study on its own. There are many types of 'enamels': gloss paint on woodwork, model paints, resin enamels for painting on metal that are cured at a temperature of 200 degrees centigrade. In fact, any hard-surfaced, shiny paint can be called 'enamel' but Vitrified enamels are actually melted glass and this is what we are discussing here. Gillie uses Vitrified enamels fused on to copper at a temperature of 850 degrees centrigrade using a kiln.

Copper comes in various gauges and thicknesses. Heavy duty tin snips are used to cut out a shape which in this instance is an oval. The finished size cannot be altered later as the copper and the glass surface become an integral whole. It is terribly important to prepare this little shape properly as any distortions will become exaggerated with repeated firings and the enamelling might 'ping' off.

The little copper oval then needs to be annealed and shaped by pummelling it with an instrument that looks like a pestle. The purpose of this tooling is to curve it slightly, like a shallow dish. This takes out all the strains at an early stage, when the copper is controllable.

The enamel comes in powder form. It looks rather like sugar that will not dissolve. It needs to have repeated washings to remove fine dust and impurities, keeping the more solid glass granules. These then have to be thoroughly mashed and mixed with distilled water. When all this has been done it will be applied with a brush, a very small amount at a time, so that the whole surface of the copper oval is gradually covered with an even layer of glass granules. This is called 'wet packing'. The water must not

Paints
(usual palette)
Vitreous oxide painting enamels, in powder form. These are ordered by number, not name, from a chart of fired colours. Gillie uses about twenty colours.

Base
Copper

Brushes
Winsor & Newton series 12, size 1. These are firm and hold a lot of paint. (Enamels dry out very quickly.) The brushes are washed frequently in alcohol and moistened with oil. They soon wear out because working in enamels is like working with fine sand.

Other materials
Small electric jeweller's kiln.
Shaping tool
Burnishing tool
Distilled water
Tissues
White carbon paper
Glass plate
Pure pine oil

create a puddle; it is drawn away with a tissue and is finally driven off gently in front of the kiln. It is then fired. The top surface is done using white and an under-surface or counter-enamel has to be laid on the reverse of the copper. This creates an enamel 'sandwich' so that the strain is taken both sides of the piece of copper.

White carbon paper is used to transfer a white outline on to the 'canvas.' Any excess is removed so that it gives just enough to see a line. Anything dark will dirty the enamel surface and could show through at the end.

Gillie likes to build up a fairly detailed background of underpainting, usually something appropriate to the sitter, so that it throws the head forward. She then puts a layer of 'opal' enamel on top of the background — the amount of opal on top determines whether it is a pale or darker colour overall, and how solid the background will appear. Nothing is worked out beforehand except the basic idea.

The silhouette, which has been left a pale bluey-white, is now concentrated on. By the time Gillie has started painting the face she is on the fifth firing. Once again she indicates the position of the basic features, copying the white carbon line. She uses a thin, pale ochre under-painting to start to work up the eyes, mouth, and so on. She works very thin but because she builds up many layers the underpainting can be covered over; if the paint was put on too thickly it could never be prevented from shining through and could remain on the surface like china painting. The sixth firing is to fuse in the first modelling of the face. If she put red (as for lips) straight on to the surface of opal enamel it would burn out and go grey, so the opal must be covered by a very fine layer of white mixed with yellow. This binds subsequent pigments and helps retain the colour of unstable ones.

The only way to learn the colour mixings of enamels is to experiment and make colour charts for your own reference. Firing changes the tones depending on the length of time the painting is in the oven. Gillie uses about twenty colours. They all mix but working in pure colours is the best method. Each colour must be ground with pure pine oil, really smoothly, on a glass plate every time it is used; if one granule has not been ground down it will show up as a blob in the final painting. It is possible to recognise the basic colours, though they are not the brilliant colour they will be when fired — they are a little powdery. The trick seems to be knowing what will kill too hot a colour, such as tan. To produce blonde hair, for instance, tan needs to be mixed with green; in fact, it looks green before it is fired. Red and yellow are the colours that are most susceptible to burning out by getting them too hot. Blue is the most dominant. Gillie puts on the 'paint' very thinly and has to watch the enamel every minute it is in the kiln to make certain she doesn't overcook it. She likes to use hatching to apply the paint: 'If you use stippling, dabbing at the surface leaving little heaps, you don't know that one of those dots may not have a grain of unmashed powder in it. It can look all right before you fire it but if it is not, complexions can look as though they are pock-marked.' The layer can also become too thick so the flow of one stroke into another is minimal; if it melts too much, it would result in a mess.

The painting is built up layer by thin layer, sometimes taking as many as twelve firings. The more often the copper returns to the kiln the more possibilities there are for it to become distorted — and the more of a risk you take. At the same time, the finer the layers and the greater the number of them the better the density, building up a three-dimensional look to the face.

One of the reasons Gillie likes enamelling her miniatures is the feeling that they are going to last and the colours will never fade. Unless they are dropped on to a hard surface or are somehow in an 850 degree centigrade fire, they will never alter. She 'loves the way it is on the surface and yet in the surface.' She has never got over the magic of putting the work in the kiln and watching it all change colour and then miraculously change back to what it should be.

Michael Coe
Watercolour on Ivorine

Michael Coe takes great care over the preparation of the surface of the base he is using. He can spend an hour or more rubbing the ivory or Ivorine with wet and dry sandpaper, with hardly any pressure, polishing it ever more finely. He inspects the surface minutely for any deep or uneven scratchmarks. When he is satisfied that it is polished to his meticulous requirements, he swabs it with ox-gall to finally degrease it and remove any remaining debris.

When he visits his subjects, he takes a large number of photographs and makes sketches at the sitting. Then, back in his studio, he studies all the information he has obtained and makes a final drawing on tracing paper.

He tapes the Ivorine to a firm base of watercolour board as this has a white surface which will shine through the Ivorine. For this he uses double-sided tape. Masking tape is also placed over the square of Ivorine to keep the area to be painted within its borders and hold it in place. The stiff support may also keep it from bowing though this would be minimal. He keeps a piece of kitchen paper under his hand, with another piece to wipe the brush on when necessary.

To trace the final sketch on to the Ivorine, he uses a 2H pencil to press with and a B pencil on the reverse. This only provides the bare outline and he then marks in the eyes, nostrils and main features. He maintains he

Paints
(usual palette)
Schmincke, artists' quality watercolours, in half-pans (tubes seem to have too much gum arabic and glycerine in them for his methods):
Yellow Ochre
Burnt Sienna
Burnt Umber
Vandyke Brown
Vermilion
Viridian
Prussian Green
Cerulean Blue
(this blue is quite a bit deeper in the Schmincke range).
French Ultramarine
Cobalt Blue
Cadmium Red
Permanent Rose
Cadmium Yellow Lemon
Neutral Tint
(sometimes also:
Brown Ochre
Raw Umber
English Red Light)

Base
Ivorine (or ivory if requested, cut to size)

Brushes
Simonart Kolinsky sable, size 000. A brush lasts him about a week of normal painting. After that, it is kept for taking the paint to the mixing palette, each colour being picked up by one brush, keeping the pans themselves perfectly clean.

Facing page
Girl with Violin, by Michael Coe.
Actual size

can end up with too much mess if he uses anything but the minimum amount of graphite: 'It's not worth it, just as much accuracy can be achieved by drawing the rest in free-hand.' The image is lined out in watercolour, using an extremely thinned-down neutral tint. To line out the more fleshy tones, he adds a small touch of violet. When he is satisfied that all the basic information is correctly in place, all the pencil is rubbed off. Where the putty eraser has been used it is carefully wiped with ox-gall to re-clean the surface. Then, using a neutral colour, he stains the base areas as a first layer, leaving the details of shading to be painted in. The lines do not show through in the finished painting as they are very pale and become broken up by layers of stippling.

Michael used to use gum arabic to dilute and make the paint smooth, but it seemed to get gummier and gummier and he discovered it could crack if it became too thick. He now uses Aquarella for dilution.

Other materials
Wet-and-dry fine sandpaper
Ox-gall
2H and B pencils
Putty eraser
Distilled water, (bought from the chemist's).
Aquarella (for watercolours on hard surfaces, or even fabrics — it stops the paint spreading).
Kitchen paper
Scalpel
Hand-held magnifying glass supported by a stand he has constructed himself.

Detail showing the accuracy with which Michael portrays the soft flesh of the girl's hand and the hard reflective surface of the wood.

1
The image is lined out by using thinned down neutral tint. Then the base areas are stained very lightly, as the first layer.

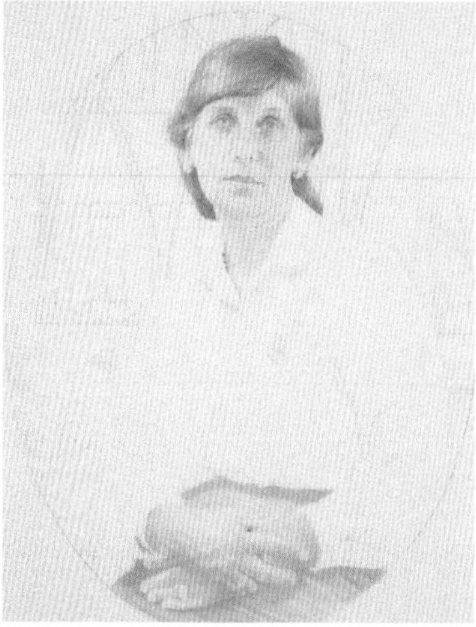

2
The hair is worked up to an almost finished state. Cobalt blue is used as underpainting for the veins and shadows, then the skin tones are applied on top.

3
Once the features are fairly well worked up, attention is given to the background, but constantly adjusting the strength of colour so the face does not appear too pale.

Mrs J. Fowler, watercolour on Ivorine by Michael Coe.
9.5 x 7.5 cm (3 3/4 x 3 in)
Michael pays as much attention to the background and clothing as he does to the face. He has to keep a constant balance in the strength of colours used so the sitter does not become overpowered by the background.

METHOD OF WORKING

Michael usually starts with the hair, working it up to an almost finished state and ensuring the brushstrokes follow precisely the direction of growth. He can spend two or three days on this before moving on to the face, starting with the eyes, then the face in general. Next he concentrates on the hands so that the skin tones are all painted together, and relate to the face.

When he begins the shading for the flesh tones he starts with Cobalt Blue. The shadows and veins are picked out first so that all the subsequent colour will go over the top, giving them the appearance of actually being under the skin. All the underpainting of the skin is in pale blue. The eyebrows are also painted fairly solidly before the warmer colours so that they do not 'look like caterpillars sitting on the top'. Children, in particular, do not usually have very prominent eyebrows and he finds this a good method of toning them down. Once the nose and the area around the eyes have been worked up, the warmer tones are applied on top. He adds Vermilion and Yellow Ochre, trying to keep the colours fairly pure, and uses tiny brush strokes. The features are modelled following the contours of the face: the brush strokes go round the chin and cheeks, away from the nose and with the line of the jaw. Michael advises that if you don't place the tiny brush strokes in the right lines you will not model the face correctly.

If the colours appear to be a bit too strong they can be washed off extremely carefully with a wet brush. On the other hand, rather than risk making a mistake, he says you can correct the situation by putting another colour on top. If the portrait is becoming too red and hot, he puts Viridian on top to cool the reds down; remember he is using such small amounts of colour on the brush that it should not build up too thickly.

Michael turns his attention to the background once the main features of face and dress are reasonably worked up. He spends as much time and effort on the background as he does on the face. Eventually the build up of colour on the background will probably mean the face appears too pale and needs more attention. The whole painting needs constant adjusting: 'You are never quite satisfied. It is always better not to add too much strength of colour too quickly. You can always add more, it is much more difficult to take it off. It takes a long time to happen. Whilst you are concentrating on one part of the painting the other sections are drying.' The layers can be hardening for several days or even a week. Subsequent layers of colour are thus going over thoroughly dry paint, making it crisper each time.

Michael tends to paint throughout the day, putting in about 9 to 10 hours on a good day. If he leaves the painting for any reason he covers it up. At night he places an old mount, covered with acid-free tissue, over the painting and puts it away it in a drawer. When he starts the day he inspects the entire surface of the painting using a lens with a strong magnification and a scalpel to lift off any minute particles of 'grit and fibre'. If the dust is loose on the surface he uses a blow brush, as you would to clean a camera lens, to disperse any particles that could clog the paint: 'If it is not done, when you paint around it it becomes more and more solid, then when you do finally scratch it off you take a bit of paint with it.' This scrutiny is a good check to see if your technique is holding up.

You may wonder how long it takes to paint a portrait in this meticulous fashion. Five to six weeks is the norm for Michael, although when he starts out he always hopes it will take less time.

Michael signs his paintings on the reverse. When he puts a finished piece in the frame he uses white backing paper cut to size so that it fits exactly inside the frame, between the backing card and the painting. He never uses white paint in his work so he relies on the strength of a pure white background to shine through the Ivorine and show the highlights.

Elizabeth Meek
Oil on Ivorine

Elizabeth Meek does the most exquisite pencil drawings and when she is painting miniatures she works from her drawings supplemented by photographs she has taken. She usually carries her camera with her wherever she goes in search of faces that appeal to her. She prefers natural light and she tries to take photographs outdoors whenever possible. She likes to spend time with the sitter, sketching and observing, looking for a particular expression or pose which most effectively portrays her subject.

Paints
(usual palette)
Rowney and/or Winsor & Newton oil paints, thinned with pure turpentine:
Flesh Tint (a very little)
Scarlet Lake
Titanium White
Burnt Sienna
Permanent Blue
Yellow Ochre
Raw Umber
Venetian Red
Ivory Black
Cadmium Red
Alizarin Crimson
Cadmium Yellow
Winsor Lemon
Prussian Blue
French Ultramarine
Viridian

Base
Ivorine

Brushes
Daler's Dalon 77, size 00000.
Winsor & Newton, series 29, spotting sable, sizes 0000, 000 and 00. Prolene, size 0000. Isabey Repique, size 00.
Elizabeth can use six different brushes per painting. The average life of brushes is two to three paintings.

Other materials
Washing-up detergent
Kitchen paper
2B pencil
Putty eraser
Pure turpentine

Left
John, oil on Ivorine by Elizabeth Meek. *Actual size*

Elizabeth works at a table with the painting flat. She cuts the Ivorine to size before she starts and cleans it with washing-up detergent to remove any greasy marks. After that she rinses it thoroughly and dries it with kitchen paper, checking there are no bits of paper left on it. From then on she is most careful not to touch the painting surface. She prefers working in daylight but finds a daylight bulb useful to extend painting-time in the winter. She is lucky in that she has good eyesight and does not need to use a magnifying glass or spectacles.

The Ivorine is not secured in any way as she likes to be free to move it around when she is working, turning the portrait whichever way she needs.

Working by eye and using a 2B pencil, she sketches an accurate outline on to the Ivorine. To help refresh her memory she has in front of her rough sketches, possibly a drawing and a carefully chosen photograph that best depicts the character of the sitter. Sometimes she will make tiny marks on the Ivorine to make sure the head is within the size limit for miniatures (50 millimetres or 2 inches maximum). If any alterations are needed the pencil is removed with a putty eraser, which can also be used to soften any too obvious 'hard' lines. This initial drawing can take up to five hours.

A very thin, light layer of appropriate colour is then put on to both the face and clothing, using light brush strokes and paint that has been well thinned with pure turpentine. Elizabeth only uses turpentine to dilute the paint as she finds linseed oil too sticky for the detail. Light and dark areas are indicated from the beginning. Even at this stage there are no areas of plain blank colour, the finished shading and colour tones are kept in mind from the beginning. This first undercoat should be left to dry for a minimum of twelve hours and could even be left to harden for a couple of days. The colour is very gradually built up with thin coats of paint until the face and hair are almost complete. For the hair Elizabeth starts with a darker base and applies the paint in continuous lines, the way the hair would grow, almost drawing with the brush. The build-up gradually becomes lighter, comprising shades such as blue, green and red. She finally creates the shine with the lightest shades.

The head alone can easily take a week, working four to five hours a day. Then the clothes and the background are worked in the same way, although she does not always paint in the same order. Elizabeth emphasizes that the background colour should always enhance the portrait rather than detract from it, and that it is a very important part of the painting: 'A background can change a picture so much.'

She finds painting miniatures a very intense occupation so she likes to regulate her painting time to about five hours a day. A portrait can take her around three weeks to complete after which she has to let it dry, ideally for about one month. She also likes to put it away for a while, to see it with fresh eyes. If she leaves a picture, even for a few minutes, she always covers it as there is dust in the air the whole time. If any dust particles do land on the painting she removes them very gently with a dry brush.

Finally the painting is taken to the framer and a sympathetic frame selected. This too can apparently take some time as the finished portrait must be a harmonious whole. Elizabeth always has her work framed under glass for protection.

Detail showing how each brush stroke follows the line of the hair.

William P. Mundy
Watercolour on Ivory and Vellum

The Golden Turban, watercolour on ivory by William P. Mundy. *Actual size*

Bill Mundy travels the world to visit his sitters. He initially photographs them in as many as thirty different poses, using a Hasselblad camera and two to three rolls of film. He lights the sitter with two large standing flash units, one high up to the front at full strength and another at head level using half-strength flash to maximise the delicate modelling of the features. Photography is necessary as no-one will sit for thirty to forty hours while he paints them. For children, he always uses three rolls of film in order to end up with three photographs good enough to base a miniature on. Detailed records of the colour of hair or eyes are made by way of pencil or watercolour sketches while the subject is still in front of him. Where possible, Bill likes to involve the sitter in choosing the best photographs, thus indicating an angle of the head or pose that is favoured. With a woman or child, he will ask them to bring two or three changes of clothing to see which they feel most comfortable in.

Bill selects about six photographs which he feels most reflect the character of the sitter, two or three of which are finally chosen as a base for the portrait. After meticulous study, a small drawing is made to the exact size of the finished portrait and is then positioned in the oval shape. If he is working on ivory, this has to be absolutely accurate as the ivory has already been cut and there is no leeway. He uses a prepared mount as a template for the correct size oval to give the dimensions for the drawing. This fine line drawing is done on thin layout paper, which enables him to transfer it to the ivory or vellum by rubbing over the back with a soft (2B or 3B) pencil and pressing through from the front with a sharp (6H) pencil or metal point. It has to be done very carefully as vellum can be permanently dented if pressed too hard;

Paints
(usual palette)
Winsor & Newton artists' quality watercolours in half pans:
Cerulean Blue
Vermilion
Alizarin Crimson
Davy's Gray
Yellow Ochre
Warm Sepia
Hooker's Green
Olive Green
Winsor Violet
Black (only for the dot of the eye)
French Ultramarine (used rarely)
White (for lace, pearls, jewellery, etc. that need highlights).
The normal technique is to paint round all white areas, leaving the ivory or vellum to show through, but now and again a picture needs 'spicing up' with tiny dots of white paint.

Base
Ivory and vellum (always ready-prepared and the ivory cut to size)

Brushes
Winsor & Newton best sable, series 7, sizes 0, 00 and 000. Even with this quality, he finds the points are not consistent.
A brush usually only lasts for one painting. When blunt he uses it on backgrounds.

Other materials
2B or 3B and 6H pencils (he sometimes uses the metal point of a compass as even a 6H pencil can become 'blunt' too quickly).
Putty eraser
Double-sided tape
Layout paper
Water to dilute

Enlargement showing the range of colours that have been used to capture the flesh tones.

any excess graphite must be removed. When he has completed this stage, he holds it up to a mirror to check it. This will show up any errors such as the eye being too high or any other feature out of proportion, which can still be corrected before he starts painting.

Bill buys ivory already prepared and cut as special tools are required to shape it. The paint would slide around on polished ivory so the surface needs to have a minute roughness, or 'tooth'. The supplier also uses a machine so that the surface is 'swept' evenly. Bill prefers not to have to touch the ready prepared surface but should it be necessary he rubs over the surface gently with a putty eraser to make sure it is free of any dirt or grease before starting work. He uses double-sided tape to secure the base to a non-flexible white surface, usually thick cardboard.

For the next stage the pencil outline is marked out faintly in Yellow Ochre on the ivory or vellum. The main features — ears, eyes, nose and mouth — are drawn in meticulously, then the hair is indicated, still using Yellow Ochre if it is blonde or brown. Other colours such as pale blue, or very pale shades of the garments themselves, are used for the clothes. The graphite residue must be completely removed with a putty eraser but there can be a snag if the paint has dried over the pencil line; it may be necessary to wash out a small part of the painted line with water and to replace it again in the exact position, because it is at this stage that the likeness commences. Bill compares it with his original drawing and the photographs (if feasible, with the sitter as well).

If the sitter has a dark enough skin tone, he will probably commence the painting with the face. Otherwise he starts with the clothes because he can tone the colours exactly to the correct strength; it is also a good way to get into a picture and Bill loves painting textures. A man's sports jacket looks almost as if it had been woven by building up the different strands of colour in paint. When he paints a silk shirt you feel you could touch it and the colours and brushwork are well worth studying. This approach to colour takes a long time. Another reason for painting the clothes and background first is to allow the face to be painted against a definite colour and tone. If it is painted only against the white of ivory or vellum the features tend to be slightly too pale.

Bill doesn't like his backgrounds to detract from the portrait; he prefers them to be complementary, to give total focus to the sitter. They are painted in fairly loosely to begin with, using Davy's Gray regardless of the final colouring he decides upon. He also favours a lilac, mixed from Winsor Violet and Davy's Gray, or perhaps some Cerulean Blue, giving a combination of three or four blended colours. This is an attempt to achieve something fairly neutral or ethereal, even wispy, unless a client specifically requests a particular background subject.

The final layers are always stippled, whatever the colouring, so the background is never one plain colour.

When the background is put in around the hair it is done very carefully, leaving the little wispy bits as untouched ivory or vellum. He outlines the hair with pale grey and applies a wash (the only wash ever used in his miniatures), loosely putting in the colours. The hair in the first instance is painted in many colours to give it vibrancy and life. Depending on the actual colour, brown for instance, the highlights are painted in using a fairly bright blue and lilac, then perhaps a hint of yellow. Later he goes over it with Yellow Ochre and Warm Sepia, slowly bringing it to a more natural colour by exaggerating all the reflected colours there are in a person's hair and giving it shine. He makes sure he follows the growth and direction of the hair with each stroke of the brush.

The face itself is built up of minute dots and lines of paint, generally following the shape and contours of the features. Bill usually starts with the ears (if they show), then the outline of the eyes, eyebrows, nose and mouth, checking the proportions constantly and making corrections, if needed, as early as possible. The colour is built up very slowly using Yellow Ochre and Vermilion in little strokes and dots — still pale, about half strength. Alizarin Crimson may be used for the cheeks. The reason he likes a hard natural surface is that it will take several layers without damage. Before he finishes the modelling, Bill often adds a highlight around the dark side of the face, at the very edge, in pale Cerulean Blue, Winsor Violet or sometimes Hooker's Green. He may also use a little of a mixture of blues or greys underneath the eyebrows perhaps with Davy's Gray to denote other areas in shadow.

When he is working on the eyes, he refers particularly to the watercolour sketches he made at the sitting. He works around the little white highlight in the eye, leaving that as untouched base ivory or vellum showing through. If the person has particularly bright sparkling eyes then he might add a tiny dot of white for added emphasis. For the eyeball itself he uses greys and blues in moderation to soften the effect.

The mouth is invariably painted last: 'I really have to concentrate on the mouth. Most of the likeness comes from a shape about 3 millimetres (1/8th inch) wide! It must be perfect. If I am listening to a play on the radio when I start to paint the mouth, I miss what is going on because my concentration is centred entirely on achieving the likeness.' He finishes the painting by working it all up to completion.

Bill keeps a photographic record of all his work, with a note on sizes, how long they took to paint and who owns them. He places the finished painting in the frame without glass and photographs it four ways — 2 1/4 inch colour transparencies, colour negatives, black and white and 35mm colour transparencies. This is to meet all possible future enquiries for newspaper articles, colour brochures or requests for samples of his work. He never allows anyone (other than the professional miniature frame maker) to take a painting out of its frame when completed because of its vulnerability to damage if handled incorrectly.

The painting is meticulously framed, in consultation with the client but usually in a traditional gold oval with a hanging ring at the top. It can be placed in a leather case with matching velvet and silk facings. Bill has on occasion been asked to include the sitter's hair in the back of the frame, in which case he asks the framer to make a special glass-backed frame and to seal it in.

Sydney Shorthouse

WATERCOLOUR ON IVORINE AND VELLUM

Sydney Shorthouse started painting miniatures after a long career in design. Characteristically, when he discovered miniatures, he researched the subject completely before attempting to paint anything. Consequently his first efforts were of as high a standard as some artists who have been painting miniatures for years. Some 70 per cent of his subjects are children, although he tries to avoid taking on commissions of children below the age of five years.

Where possible Sydney prefers to meet and talk to the subject, getting to know something about them, before taking a series of photographs. This is very professionally done, using a 35 mm film, a tripod and a remote control shutter release. The lighting comes from a 500 watt photo-flood lamp with a brolly diffuser. The film is then developed into a sheet of contact prints from which about four photographs are selected. Standard size prints are then made from these, to enable a final choice of just one 25 x 20 millimetre (10 x 8 inch) print, which will be the basis of the portrait.

The piece of Ivorine he is going to use is cut into a rectangle 6 millimetres (¼ inch) wider and taller than the maximum extent of the oval. The same size rectangle is then cut out of a piece of card and the Ivorine set into this space so that it is flush with the surface. If it requires packing to bring it level with the surface the underneath paper has to be white or ivory because it will show through. The Ivorine base is rubbed with a small amount

PAINTS
(usual palette)
Winsor & Newton artists' quality watercolours in tubes, (he feels they stay fresher):
Light Red
Flesh Tint
Alizarin
Viridian
Scarlet Lake
French Ultramarine plus whatever other colours are needed for clothes, hair, etc. He uses Winsor Blue, turned to green with Yellow Ochre and Sepia to create soft varied backgrounds.

BASE
Ivorine or vellum

BRUSHES
Winsor & Newton best sable, series 7, size 000. These last for a couple of paintings in good condition and are then relegated for use on backgrounds.

OTHER MATERIALS
Talcum powder
Tissues
Kitchen paper
Clear acetate film
2B pencil
Putty eraser
Needle (in a holder)
Scalpel knife
Water to dliute

Facing page
Loraine, portrait of the artist's wife. Watercolour on Ivorine. *Actual size*

of talcum powder, using kitchen paper, to degrease it. Any loose powder must be completely removed. Sydney keeps a supply of kitchen paper by him; this is folded in half and used for wiping and resting wet brushes on.

Sydney takes meticulous care 'mapping out' before he starts painting. He uses an acetate grid made up of approximately twenty-four squares to transfer the subject from the chosen photograph in 2B pencil on to the Ivorine. This is done by marking off the same number of reduced grid lines to create smaller squares, marked out very faintly across the face of the Ivorine. The glass for the intended frame is placed over the grid and the oval shape traced on to the Ivorine.

He uses pale French Ultramarine to paint in the outline. When he is content that he has captured the image, the pencil lines are rubbed out with a putty eraser. After that, if he feels it is too strong anywhere, he very gently damps down the French Ultramarine outline. He then washes in the skin tones, leaving the highlights; the basic hair tone is also washed in before starting work on the head. The edges of the shadowed areas are softened and then worked into the adjoining area with fine brushwork. Sydney always starts with the eyes, bringing them to almost the finished state before proceeding to the other facial features. He builds up the tones by applying tiny dots of colour. For shadows he uses Light Red and French Ultramarine or Winsor Violet in varying strengths according to the depth. Once he is satisfied that a good likeness has been achieved, he can turn his attention to the clothes and background.

The Ivorine is finally cut out with scissors to the previously drawn oval shape so that it fits the frame perfectly. Sydney takes immense care to present his work beautifully framed, using a gold oval set in a velvet background to match the colours in the painting. If the client wishes, the oval can be set in a leather case.

1
Sydney takes great care 'mapping out' before the painting is begun. He uses an acetate grid made up of approximately 24 squares to transfer the subject from the photograph on to the Ivorine. The corresponding squares allow him a highly accurate placing of all the features.

2
Starting with the eyes, Sydney tries to bring them to an almost finished state before proceeding downwards to the nostrils and then upwards to the brow. He arrives at the skin tones by applying tiny dots of colour, similar to those you would see in a highly magnified section of a colour photograph in a magazine. The skin tones are made up of Light Red, French Ultramarine and Winsor Violet in varying strengths, always building up the shape by deepening shadows and creating highlights. He tries to complete this stage in one working session.

3
Once Sydney is satisfied that he has achieved a good likeness he will turn his attention to the clothes and background. He maintains that it could be a terrible waste of time working on these in detail before you know that the portrait itself is going to be alright.

Enlargement of the portrait of **Loraine** (8.5 x 6.5cm / 3½ x 3in) by Sydney Shorthouse. Notice the attention to detail in the Paisley pattern on her dress.

Landscape
acrylic on Bristol board
by Jo Dollemore

Actual size

Landscapes

Jo Dollemore

Acrylic on Bristol Board or Paper

Jo Dollemore does a lot of walking around her local area, taking her camera with her, and her inspiration comes from this scenery. She works from photographs which she has taken herself and she now has quite a collection.

For miniature work she always starts with a fresh palette, making sure everything is absolutely clean as dust particles seem to come from nowhere. These days she paints sitting at an upright easel as she has had a lot of neck trouble, and works for about seven hours a day. She finds Bristol board benefits from a wash of acrylic paint over all the surface to seal it before she starts painting. This enables further washes to flow more easily, which is the main problem with a surface that facilitates crisp detail. She adds a very slightly pink tone to the wash as it gives a warm atmosphere to the finished painting. She also works a little pink into the sky near the horizon because trees look better with a slightly pink background. The sky must be completely finished before any trees or hedges are put in.

In general Jo uses much the same method as she does for larger work. After the background of pale pink she sketches in the main details very lightly in pencil. The important areas are then blocked in in pale versions of their final colours. Next she puts in the sky. If there is a relatively large area of sky she makes it as interesting as possible, otherwise it is kept fairly pale and plain. She advises: 'You have to be careful not to make the sky too strong as acrylic can tend to dry slightly darker.' For summer paintings she sometimes adds a touch of green and in winter a spot of Raw Sienna, both in very small quantities. She tries never to touch the sky once the rest of the painting is begun.

Distant trees are dabbed in to start with, using a dry hog's hair brush. Then she loads a watercolour brush and 'rolls' the paint off the point to do the detail of winter trees in the foreground. The whole of the painting is gradually built up with more and more detail. She has no rules when she paints but she has quite a few useful

Paints
(usual palette)
Artists' quality acrylics:
French Ultramarine Blue
Cobalt Blue
Sap Green
Azo Yellow
Crimson
Cadmium Red
Quinacridone Violet
Raw Sienna
Burnt Umber
Titanium White
(She has been using acrylics for thirty years and, having tried most other media, she now uses acrylics exclusively.)

Base
Bristol board or watercolour paper
(Although she says she is still looking for the perfect ground).

Brushes
Cotman, series 3 or Winsor & Newton, Sceptre Gold, sizes 2-5. She generally prefers larger brushes (size 5) with a good point and rarely uses smaller than a size 2. Small hog's hair brush for 'dabbing in.'

Other materials
Pencil
Water to dilute
Optivisor

1
The Bristol board is given a thin wash of paint to seal the surface so as to facilitate further washes of colour when blocking in the main shapes of the landscape. The features, such as trees, are put in in pencil but the outlines are kept to a minimum.

2
The hedgerows begin to take shape, with branches appearing on the trees and some depth to the landscape. Detail is gradually built up over the whole painting.

3
Shadows are left to the last to give depth and interest. Then the final touches can bring it all to life, increasing the sense of distance by focusing the foreground.

Enlargement of Jo Dollemore's **Landscape**. Although Jo paints larger works in much the same style she is able to successfully adapt her subject matter and working practices to miniatures.

tips. One is not to mix more than three colours together as they tend to become muddy. Keeping the colours a lighter shade is another. She emphasizes that shadows are very important. They must be carefully observed as they can greatly change the way the painting looks. Don't paint them in too soon, leave them for as long as possible as they can be useful for improving the composition. She uses an optivisor (magnifying lenses worn like goggles) when she starts to put in the detail, but otherwise she tries to keep a distance when she is blocking in the initial features. She thinks it is a mistake to use too small a brush, you just need one with a good point that holds plenty of paint.

Robert Hughes
Oil on Board

PAINTS
(usual palette)
Winsor & Newton artists' quality oil paints:
Ivory Black
Raw Umber
Burnt Umber
Burnt Sienna
Yellow Ochre
Cadmium Yellow Light
Titanium White
Cerulean Blue
Ultramarine Blue
Terre Verte

BASE
Smooth side of primed hardboard

BRUSHES
Winsor & Newton sable, series 7, sizes 000-2. This preference has a lot to do with the shape and weight of the handle. A selection of small hog's hair brushes, 1 stroke sable.

OTHER MATERIALS
White primer
Liquin (for dilution)
White spirit
Needle
A rag for wiping anything and everything (it rests on his lap like a napkin).
Retouching varnish

Robert Hughes makes painting miniature landscapes in oils look easy but then he has had a lot of practice. He has tremendous powers of concentration when he is working and seems to paint with effortless ease. He works from photographs when he is doing commissions but otherwise he is perfectly capable of painting lovely little scenes of the local countryside from memory.

Robert works sitting at a table, with the board held flat between his fingers. He has brushes in many shapes and types of bristle and he always lays his paints out on the palette in the same order, as listed above right. Despite his seemingly inspirational method of putting on the paint, everything is carefully worked out with regard to the space he is to fill. He has all his boards cut to size to fit a selection of frames that are all ready to be assembled. Whilst the work is progressing he sometimes places the frame over the painting to check that all is well and to get an idea of how it will look when finished.

Left
Chilton Foliat, by Robert Hughes.
Actual size
Robert always puts a light layer of retouching varnish on the finished painting but advises that it should have a final varnish applied six months later, when it has dried thoroughly.

Detail of centre of painting. Robert likes to work very fast, totally absorbed in pushing the paint around until the scene comes to life. He puts in the highlights last, using the lightest tones of paint or even scratching paint off with a needle – as he has done here for the window, water-line and some twigs.

First Robert draws in a minimal sketch on the primed board and then proceeds to block in the various areas of colour. He always starts with the sky. Using a flat sable brush he quickly and deftly sweeps back and forth. His favourite blues for the sky are Cerulean Blue and Ultramarine Blue mixed with white, and a touch of another colour for the changing seasons, such as Burnt Sienna for early spring. The hedges and distant trees are 'scumbled' in with a small hog's hair brush to begin with. A lot of the colour mixing is done on the painting. Then, using a finer sable brush, he proceeds to put in the detail. He mixes the paint straight from the tube, thinning it with Liquin only when he needs glazes.

Alois Majzlik began his artistic career painting murals and stage sets in Czechoslovakia and Yugoslavia.

Alois Majzlik
Oil on Copper

Paint
(usual palette)
Winsor & Newton or Rowney artists' quality oil paints:
Zinc White
Lemon Yellow
Yellow Ochre
Cobalt Blue (for skies)
Emerald Green (mixed with yellow)
Verde Naturale
Viridian and sometimes a little Carmine.
(He never uses black.)

Base
Copper sheet

Brushes
Sable watercolour brushes, sizes 0, 1 and 2. He prefers a longer haired brush which he trims down as it wears out to suit his own requirements.

Other materials
Linseed oil
Pure turpentine
Clear matt varnish
Silver sealant

Alois Majzlik began his artistic career painting murals and stage sets in Czechoslovakia and Yugoslavia. Although he started working on such a large scale he went on to become one of the world's leading miniaturists.

Ideally Alois prefers to paint on location but finds it is extremely difficult to do really detailed work this way. People, traffic, weather and dust getting into the paint make it almost impossible. He makes sketches and, if it is a quiet place, he will start the basic drawing and painting. Once the rough stage is completed however, he returns to his studio.

Alois paints on copper sheet cut to size, prepared and cleaned thoroughly in advance. He finds that copper provides an ideally smooth and durable base for oil paints. He then applies a smooth coat of white oil paint as a primer. The back should also be sealed as copper can corrode after a while. He normally uses a metal sealant for this but says varnish will do. If the glow of pink copper is required to give the finished painting a certain

Left
Scotney Castle, by Alois Majzlik.
Actual size
Alois likes to paint on copper sheet since it provides an ideally smooth and durable base for oil paints as well as giving a warm tone to the finished painting.

In this detail you can see clearly Alois' method of applying small amounts of paint to the surface.

look, the painting surface can be primed with varnish; it must be allowed to harden before the painting starts.

He gently draws in the basic outlines on to the white primed surface in pencil, then blocks in blank areas of colour roughly but lightly. Mistakes can still be corrected at this early stage. His basic method of applying paint is the same as any other oil painter's but on a smaller scale. He thins his paint with a mix of three-quarters linseed oil to one-quarter pure turpentine. The work is built up gradually, picking up small amounts of paint. As with any oil painting, the finest highlights of light and shade go in last.

Alois can work for hours without stopping and is sometimes still in his studio in the early hours of the morning. When the finished painting is dry, he gives it a coat of clear matt varnish. The frames he has made up in advance, keeping a selection of his three or four favourite mouldings in a cupboard.

Vivien Mullett
Watercolour on Paper

Vivien likes the 'grand scene', the big views — mountains and water, landscapes without people in them are the subjects that excite her. Yet she paints some of the smallest paintings, usually about 35 x 50 millimetres (1 1/2 x 2 inches). When enlarged, every detail is there. She is one of those artists whose painting I would like to magnify until it became very much larger to see if it still worked. I rather suspect it would.

She paints sitting at a table, with the work supported on a slight slope, a magnifying glass in one hand and her brush in the other. All her paints, paraphernalia and photographs are to hand. She is beginning to experience some back trouble and is thinking of ways to raise her working surface so that she sits more upright. She lives and works in London and plans her holidays so she that can visit wild, mountainous regions to soak up the scenery she loves. She always takes her camera and uses many rolls of film. She picks a subject or view with which she feels she has an affinity yet at the same time gives her a good composition to work on. Since they are places she has been to, she can remember what it was like being there and she is not merely copying the photograph. More than just the geography is retained in her mind.

She decides what size the painting will be and which part of the selected photograph she is going to use. Sometimes it is the whole of it, just as she saw it through the viewfinder, at other times part of it is cut out as she selects a good composition. She draws straight on to the paper very lightly with an 0.3 propelling pencil which is hard but very fine. Occasionally she goes over this with a faint wash outline but that method doesn't always work. The pencil can be rubbed out if something goes wrong but the paint is not so easy to remove.

Paints
(usual palette)
Various makes of artists' quality watercolours, mainly Winsor & Newton, in tubes:
Payne's Gray ('a real chameleon' that mixes with anything)
Cobalt Blue
Sap Green
Leaf Green
Alizarin Crimson
Blue Black (rather than black)
Raw Umber
Burnt Umber
Indigo
Cerulean Blue
Cyanine Blue (a good transparent blue)
Antwerp Blue
Cadmium Yellow Light
Schmincke:
Cadmium Red
Permanent Violet (very rich colours)
Rotring White; laid down very thinly, for example to give light under leaves.

Base
Arches hot pressed watercolour paper.

Left
River Scene, by Vivien Mullett.
Actual size
Vivien paints the largest scenes in the smallest areas and yet you feel that if they were enlarged to 3 feet by 5 feet they would still look as though you could walk into them.

laying a basic wash and then working into it if it is to be cloudy. Vivien explains: 'The sky can take quite a lot of detailed attention . . . If that does not work then the rest of the painting will not come out right either.' The sky is a 'pivot point' and she may scrap the work if she is dissatisfied with it. She generally progresses in sections on the rest of the landscape, continuing until one part is complete before starting on the next. For example, after finishing the sky she might turn her attention to the mountains. Then she works forward into the foreground, washing into it to get some gradual idea of the tones.

Every painting is different so it is impossible to generalise about the order of work. Trees, bushes, rocks and other details are put in with amazing intensity: 'You feel you are drawing with the brush, it's not really stippling, although you are using such a small amount of paint. You need to show what is happening, to make it believable, so that you can walk into the painting.' Vivien almost indicates every leaf with each tiny stroke of applied paint. This is where the Rotring white ink, laid down extremely thinly, can provide a smooth non porous underpainting base, making the paint applied on top in those areas really crisp; it can also be scratched off. Paint put over the top increases in transparency and gives a lovely light effect, almost a glow, like the sunshine on a leaf.

The most focal thing is done last. Often this is the water and getting the 'texture' or surface right is crucial: 'There is a lot of colour in water and a tremendous amount going on.'

Vivien's advice to people who are trying to master miniatures on such a small scale is to be patient, to proceed at a pace you can work at and to really get in to the subject. Observation is all-important: 'You can tell when people have just painted things superficially and they have not really looked into it. As to knowing when to stop, you just go on until you cannot do any more.' Rosalind Pierson does a lot

Brushes
Winsor & Newton, series 29, size 000, spotting sable, size 000. Humbrol model painting brush, size 000 (inexpensive but keeps its point very well). She likes Winsor & Newton's designer sable brushes, series 3A and will use series 7, size 2, for washes but otherwise their brushes do not work so well for her when laying in a wash as they don't seem to let go of the paint.

Other materials
0.3 Pentel propelling pencil.
Water to dilute

1
The painting is done in sections starting with the sky. It sets the tone for the rest of the painting.

2
Each section is worked up to an almost finished state before proceeding to the next. Generally the foreground is last.

3
At this stage the highlights have been added to the trees and the entire back and middle grounds finished leaving the river, as the focal point, to be worked on last. Paint is still patiently built up in tiny brush strokes even though it is filling a comparatively large expanse of water.

Detail of the finished work showing the many colours in the reflections and disturbance to the water.

Rosalind Pierson

Watercolour on Bristol Board

Rosalind Pierson does a lot of groundwork through the viewfinder of a camera. She is extremely selective and fastidious about her compositions, and she will take several rolls of film to achieve one or two photographs that she is satisfied with and willing to use. Dartmoor is her favourite area and she will walk all day searching for the right light, wanting to depict those vast skies and spaces in all their different aspects and yet do so in a miniature.

Rosalind prefers to work on a flat table and if there is no daylight, she uses a 'daylight bulb' in a lamp. She has recently started to use a magnifying glass to try to improve her brushwork.

The first outlines are drawn in very vaguely using pencil, with the most accuracy and attention concentrated on the predominant features. Then she starts to apply the colour by putting in the sky. In the main she relies on uncluttered skies to focus on the landscape. Some of her cold, clear aquamarine and yellow winter skies are breathtaking.

She then continues to the middle and foregrounds where she mostly uses stippling. For the middle distances, she occasionally dabs paint off with a moist tissue. The intensity of this varies depending on the degree of the required result; it lightens and softens, taking the colour out and blurring the stippling slightly. She can also fractionally lighten a whole area by using a soft eraser.

Paints

(usual palette)
Mainly Winsor & Newton, artists' quality watercolour paints, in half-pans:
Lemon Yellow
New Gamboge
Yellow Ochre
Viridian
Sap Green
Cobalt Blue
Intense Blue (transparent and powerful)
Burnt Umber
Indian Red
Burnt Sienna
Payne's Gray
She seems to collect blues and greens, some of which are Schmincke paints.

Base

Bristol board
(This used to be a heavily clay-filled board that provided a very smooth finish, but because it cracked when handled in full size sheets the suppliers gave up producing it. Now it has come to mean a lightweight, ultra-smooth-surfaced board that has good colour acceptance and can tolerate erasure without damage to the surface. Its disadvantage is that it is difficult to apply a wash.)

Left
Winter Landscape, by Rosalind Pierson. *Actual size*
The only time a wash is used is to paint a clear sky that beautifully emphasizes the bare trees which are drawn in, almost to the last twig, using the point of a sable brush.

The reason for these blending methods is to achieve overall harmony of form, particularly for the middle distance and background. The trees seem to be painted by drawing in the finest twig with the brush. For added textural emphasis Rosalind has a method of drawing a nearly dry brush, fully charged with paint, across a previously stippled area so that more paint catches on the surface: 'Stippling alone is the purest way to lay on colour but if the stippling is too regular it creates an artificial look and the landscape is no longer real. The brushwork must relate to what is being painted and vary accordingly; leaves on a tree would not be treated in the same way as ripples on a stream.'

When painting the more salient features Rosalind works on many different areas, constantly balancing the light and shade in each section. Since she uses no white, the surface of the paper provides the lightest areas and if it is not left clear enough some paint must be removed. This can only be done to a slight extent or the surface of the paper will be roughened, so care has to be taken right from the start.

Rosalind prefers to frame her paintings 'large', sometimes ending up with an overall frame and mount size that is about 180 x 125 millimetres (7 x 5 inches) even though the size of the painting is no more than 50 x 75 millimetres (2 x 3 inches). When she is tackling the wide open spaces of moorlands, this certainly seems to suit her work better than it would looking claustrophobic in a small metal frame.

Brushes
Winsor & Newton sable, series 16, size 000, and series 12, size 00. Her criteria for a perfect brush are that it must have a good point and enough body to hold plenty of paint. She likes a 'broken-in' series 16 best.

Other materials
Pencil
Soft eraser
Tissues
Magnifying glass

Detail showing how the handling of the brushwork relates to the trees, the snow on the bank and the water.

Sheila Sanford
WATERCOLOUR ON VELLUM

Sheila Sanford paints many of her scenes from the countryside around her home. If you are ever in that part of the world you suddenly start noticing little Sheila Sanford views all around you. A narrow country lane winding through high banks of wild flowers or a field gate that looks oddly familiar make you smile in recognition.

Sheila's workplace is next to the window but she also uses a daylight lamp. She props her board up on a piece of wood making a slope at a comfortable angle. She also uses an ordinary small plastic magnifying glass whilst she is painting. She works mainly from photographs, but unlike other artists we have already mentioned, she doesn't mind how bad they are as they are only referred to for specific information. They are used more as an *aide-mémoire* rather than as the basis for her actual paintings.

Sheila starts by making a sketch on to tracing paper, and traces it down on to the vellum by rubbing over the back of another sheet of tracing paper with soft pencil and then going over the front with a tapestry needle stuck into a wooden bobbin to make a handle. This gives a really fine line from the tracing. Any unwanted pencil lines can be rubbed out after the painting is completed.

Sheila has a thoroughly proven method of making sure that her work is secure and protected at all times. The vellum (or whatever base she is using) is taped down around the edge, on to a board that has been covered with white paper, which in turn has been completely covered in sellotape (see diagram on page 31). The tracing paper can be firmly secured with tape for tracing off the sketch and removed at will, or kept for accurate checking of the composition. This then has a working

PAINTS
(usual palette)
Winsor & Newton artists' quality watercolours, in half-pans:
Cadmium Yellow
Burnt Umber
Raw Sienna
Scarlet Lake
Alizarin
Viridian
Winsor Blue
Payne's Gray,
Occasionally:
Aurora Yellow
Raw Umber
Permanent Rose
Winsor Violet
Hooker's Green
Cobalt Blue
Neutral Tint
Designer's gouache
Laser White.

BASE
Vellum (Kelmscott)
She also uses Ivorine and paper.

BRUSHES
Winsor & Newton sable, series 7, sizes 000-2.

OTHER MATERIALS
Ox-gall
Gum arabic
Distilled water
Tissues
Small plastic magnifying glass.
Tracing paper,
Tapestry needle
Soft pencil

Left
Landscape, by Sheila Sanford.
Actual size.
Sheila's delight in nature is reflected in her composition. Your eye is pulled back and forth between the bright pink flowers in the foreground to the tallest dark branches of the trees, wanting to savour it all.

mount put over it and another piece of card over the whole. Even if the phone rings or she is momentarily distracted, the work can be covered and kept safe with the least amount of difficulty.

To lay a wash on to vellum, which can be difficult, she uses ox-gall mixed neat into the paint on the palette. Ox-gall aids the flow and 'wetability' of the paint. She also adds a few drops of gum arabic to the water used to wet the brush for putting on the rest of her paints and she uses distilled water for anything that is applied to the painting.

Her technique is based on the usual watercolour principle that the white of the ground is left to shine through where the most light is needed. She also uses white gouache for any highlights that are needed towards the end, or where they have been missed. First she fills the whole space with tentative colour, almost blocking in, but very pale. She builds up from there, adding more and more detail as she goes along. She has a way of putting a bush or flower very close up in the foreground that gives a feeling of distance to the view on the horizon.

'To think small is important when doing a miniature. It is good because you can paint in every twig and not be told off for it. You really get into the detail of it.'

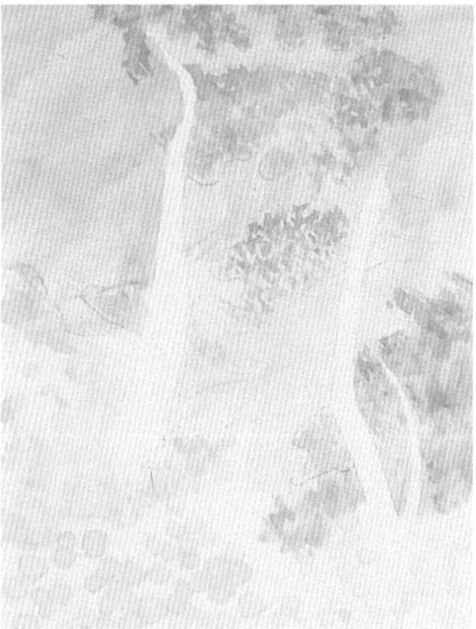

1
'Having worked out the composition on tracing paper, I transferred the drawing to the support, which in this case is vellum. I did a very tentative painting, marking with blobs where the rhododendrons would be and then washing in the sky and leaving the trunks of the trees white.'

2
'I went round each of the flowers with green, then a pale wash of Burnt Umber, used Raw Sienna on the trunks, and then darkened the leaves of the trees.'

3
'I did more work on the leaves of the trees and painted in some darker branches. The rhododendrons were developed by giving them some shape and the leaves darkened in places and at the same time I painted round some branches and twigs in the bush. Pale pine cones were painted in on the lower branches on the left.'

Enlargement of the final stage shows the strength of Sheila's style of painting given that the original measures just 6.2 x 4.9 cm ($2\frac{1}{2}$ x 2 in).

Painswick Post Office
by Eric Morton

Actual size

ARCHITECTURE

Eric Morton

WATERCOLOUR ON PAPER

When Eric Morton paints a wall every brick is painted individually. He also has a gift for making square, rather awkward compositions into paintings that people want to own. He paints beautiful landscapes which nearly always have a building in them somewhere. He also has a talent for steam trains not to mention a few other subjects!

He always takes a photograph but he likes to do a sketch as well if possible. The time or situation can make this difficult as, for example, when he is leaping about in the street in the middle of London looking for an angle. He walks round and round a building trying to find an interesting composition where the light is as he wants it. Sunlight is desirable as he likes strong shadows.

PAINTS
(usual palette)
Winsor & Newton and Rowney artists' quality watercolours, in half pans and tubes:
Cadmium Red
Alizarin Crimson
Cadmium Yellow
Raw Sienna
Burnt Umber
Viridian
Olive Green
Cobalt Blue
Cerulean Blue
French Ultramarine
Payne's Gray
Neutral Tint
He does not necessarily stick to one make, but looks for the most lightfast pigments that will suit his purpose.

BASE
Schoellershammer 90 gsm hot-pressed paper.
Schoellershammer also do a very silky smooth surfaced board, supplied by Frisk.

BRUSHES
Winsor & Newton sable, series 12, sizes 000 - 1.
He likes the shorter bristle for more control. These brushes will do two to three paintings before they deteriorate.

Enlarged section of Painswick Post Office. When looking at Eric's work there are never any jarring elements because the perspective is always perfectly drawn.

When he gets back home Eric draws the composition out on drafting film. It is then turned over and marked out on the back, drawing along the essential lines in pencil. He attaches the drafting film securely to the board to which he has already attached his paper. Using a 6H pencil, he very lightly draws the sketch so that it marks the paper underneath. For a particularly complicated subject, he makes corresponding registration marks on both the paper and the film so that he can reposition it later if necessary. Any mistake or too much graphite on the paper is rubbed away with a putty eraser. He then draws in the outline with a brush, using very pale Raw Sienna. When it has all been carefully noted in this way he can erase the pencil altogether.

He starts painting by blocking in with pale colour washes as near in tone to the finished colour as he can anticipate. The sky must be completed first, but it can be tricky getting a good wash. The cloud effects are achieved by lifting colour off rather than putting it on. This needs to be done quickly, before the paint can dry.

His next preoccupation is with the building or the main feature. He works on various parts of the painting,

Left
Mr Fortnum & Mr Mason, by Eric Morton. *Actual size*
When Eric paints a building, no matter how small the scale, he paints every brick.

keeping a balance with the background. The whole is built up with stippling, short strokes and fine lines; he adds a drop of gum arabic to the water and paints fairly dry. The Dr Martin's white is usually for the highlights towards the end but he also uses it for an opaque pastel effect. If he needs to remove any paint he uses a scalpel blade, out of its holder, so that he can control it with the lightest touch. It must be really sharp and used very delicately so as not to destroy the surface of the paper.

Eric prefers to do all his painting in daylight but sometimes, when working to a deadline, he has to resort to an artificial daylight bulb. However, he will only do this when most of the colour is already laid down. He also uses a head visor magnifier. His advice is: 'Never put too much colour on. Do not concentrate too much on one part. Try to stand back from the painting from time to time as there is a danger when you are concentrating so intensely that the section you are working on becomes over-emphasized.'

One of the things he is vehement about is his responsibility to the purchasers of his work. He uses acid-free board for all aspects of mounting and framing, the best watercolour paper he can buy and lightfast pigments. 'I consider that if a person is willing to pay a considerable sum of money for one of my paintings then they should be able to expect it to last.'

Other materials
- Washing-up detergent
- Double-sided tape
- White spirit
- Gum arabic
- Dr Martin's White (smooth and dense).
- Scalpel blade
- Drafting film
- 6H pencil
- Putty eraser
- Head visor magnifier
- Palette knife

Detail from the Fortnum and Mason clock.

Strawberries
by Sheila Fairman

Actual size

Still Life

Sheila Fairman

Oil on Ivorine

Sheila Fairman is a very versatile artist who excels at almost any subject but hardly ever thinks her work is good enough. Her paintings have a lovely sense of humour. She likes to paint things as they are, wormholes and all. She enthuses about texture and cakes are still her first love: fairly solid looking cake with sugar on top, currants and cherries with the light shining through, and many lovely contrasts. Fruit probably come next in her list of favourite subjects.

To prepare for a painting, she washes the Ivorine by rubbing it with washing-up detergent then makes sure it is thoroughly clean and dry. She has already completed a detailed tonal sketch of her subject, the same size as it will be on the Ivorine. She says: 'You should pay as much attention to the spaces as the subject matter, they are just as important to the painting.' The sketch will be placed under the Ivorine and the main outlines marked on to the surface. Meanwhile a white background board of thick card is prepared using four small rectangles of double-sided tape. These are stuck in the middle of where each of the four sides of the piece of Ivorine will be. The top is peeled back from the tape and re-stuck over the sticky part that protrudes from under the Ivorine, when it is in place. This allows the sketch to be inserted and the painting to be removed easily when it is finished, and stops her hand sticking to the tape while she is working.

The outlines are drawn in, using the correct colours as they will appear in the finished work mixed with Titanium White: 'They must always be mixed with white

Detail showing how Sheila has captured different forms and textures, from the succulent quality of the strawberries to the unyielding weave of the wicker basket.

Paints
(usual palette)
Oil paints, artists' quality (it does not matter so much about the make):
Titanium White
Burnt Sienna
Burnt Umber
Yellow Ochre
Raw Sienna
Indian Yellow (a gorgeous colour for glazing the top of currant buns)
Alizarin
Bright Red
Ultramarine
Cerulean
Sap Green
Cadmium Yellow
She also has a range of colours for flowers which she says have to be the purest you can find.

Base
Ivorine

Brushes
Best Kolinsky sable, any make, as long as it has a good point. Size 1 and occasionally size 0. A small flat nylon brush.

Other materials
White spirit
Palette knife
Tissues

1
Using a size 1 sable brush, which holds a reasonable amount of paint, the main objects are blocked in. The Chelsea bun was done in Burnt Sienna, very thin and transparent. The pattern was marked out and the top built up using more layers of Burnt Sienna, Burnt Umber to mark out the pattern and a minute amount of Alizarin to give a glow. The cherry cake was tackled next, Burnt Sienna again but following on with Yellow Ochre and Raw Sienna, 'a nice transparent colour'. The cherries were marked in in red, very faintly because red is a colour with remarkable staining power. The paper case was blocked in with Ultramarine, Burnt Sienna and Titanium white.

2
The currants were added to the Chelsea bun using Ultramarine and Burnt Umber; some have more brown in them, others are quite dark.

3
The sugar on the Chelsea bun is Ultramarine, a little bit of Alizarin and Titanium White because sugar is never really white. The crumbs are placed to give interest to the composition. The cherries are brought up to strength with glazes of Alizarin and Bright Red. The light shines through them, which means that they will be light on the opposite side from the main light source. Finally Sheila puts in a tiny white highlight on the cherry in the foreground. 'The light is the most important thing and all these little touches, carefully observed, lift the painting and give it life.'

4
The background is done last. The shadows are a very important part of the composition – there are a lot of reflected colours in shadows, which can make all the difference. In this painting there is quite a bit of Burnt Sienna glowing through.
Actual size 11 x 15.7 cm (4 1/4 x 6 in)

to prevent staining. This exercise gets the position right, which is terribly important.' The sketch is then stuck above the painting to act as a guide as it progresses. Mistakes at this early stage can be wiped off with white spirit. Later on, paint can be carefully scratched off with a palette knife, when it is dry.

All Sheila's paintings are built up in transparent layers of thin paint. The paint is mixed straight from the tube and not thinned down. She cleans her brushes with white spirit and uses her paints fresh and soft.

Sheila's favourite background colour is a mixture of Yellow Ochre and Titanium White. She advises that you mix sufficient quantities before you start, to avoid running out before the area is completed. She applies the paint with a small flat nylon brush until she is close to the part already worked. Then she uses a size 1 brush to fill in close to the edges and in the shadows, literally holding the brush upright and dabbing down gently. Paper tissues are used to blot off excess paint during the progress of work and always after the final application of the background colour. This removes any unwanted brush marks and gives a smooth, delicate finish.

Elaine Fellows
Watercolour on Vellum

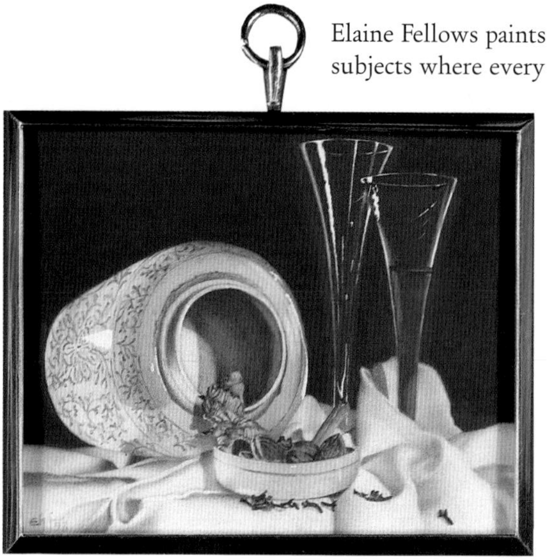

Elaine Fellows paints the most exquisite still life subjects where every detail of a piece of lace or the pattern on a porcelain vase is perfect. Her work invokes a rich atmosphere of bygone days and nostalgia. For costumed portraits she asks her sitters to wear period garments, which brings a tremendous sense of authenticity to the painting. Some of her paintings look like minuscule Old Masters although none is a copy of any existing painting.

To paint a still life, Elaine sets up the composition at the correct distance and level to show her the surfaces and lighting she needs. When she painted a large brass ewer, for instance, she found she preferred to look up at it slightly so she raised it by putting blocks on the shelf, under a cloth and treated the levels of the other objects accordingly. She likes strong colours and strong contrasts and so tends to choose objects with contrasting surfaces: matt ginger next to shiny porcelain for example.

The lighting is also important. She does a lot of work at night: 'Working at home can sometimes be very difficult with constant interruptions. At night everything calms down and you can shut yourself away but of course the daylight has gone by then.' She draws the curtains even in daylight and sets up spotlights to give her the deep, dramatic shadows, reflections and bright sparkles at which she excels. It takes her two to three weeks to complete a painting but she has the security that the subject won't go away or change.

The vellum is already treated and cut to size when she buys it. The first thing she does is stick it down on to

Paints
(usual palette)
Winsor & Newton artists' watercolours, in tubes that have gone hard
Lamp Black
Vandyke Brown
Burnt Umber
Gamboge Yellow
China White
Vermilion
French Ultramarine
Cobalt Blue
Rose Madder
These are the basics though there are others.

Base
Vellum
(Kelmscott, grade A)

Brushes
Winsor & Newton sable, series 16, sizes 00 and 1 for painting and size 7 for backgrounds (unless it is stippled, when she will use a smaller brush on which the point has worn out).

Other materials
Gold leaf
Scalpel
Scissors
Magnifying glass
Black outlining pen
Pencils
Size 8 sable for brushing off pumice.

Left
Spicing the Wine,
by Elaine Fellows. Elaine is excited by contrasts of surfaces and strong light is essential for showing this well. The deep velvety backgrounds are built up of three layers of paint to provide a good foil to the subject matter.

backing board. This board can be foam-core photoboard for her slightly larger work, but for miniatures she uses playing cards. This card has a waxy film or coating on it so she goes over the surface with pumice stone to remove the coating, which removes the printing as well: 'It gives a good grip to the surface you put the glue on to.' It is the pattern side she removes, leaving the 'suit' side showing. She likes to feel she is emulating Nicholas Hilliard in this — his portraits were stuck to playing cards for support. She now uses photomount to bond the card as it gives flexibility of movement. Once stuck, the vellum and card are put in a book press (or under heavy books) until they are dry, set and perfectly flat.

Meanwhile Elaine sits and sketches the arranged still life in pencil, on thin paper. The drawing is outlined with black pen when she is satisfied that the information is correct. Then the tracing of all the essential positional lines is transferred to the surface of the vellum, using a 6H pencil. She puts pumice powder on the vellum just before she starts applying the paint, just to make sure any grease is removed. At the same time it also removes some of the pencil, lightening the lines. The pumice is dusted on with cottonwool and brushed off with a large sable brush, which also ensures there is no grit of any kind left on the surface. Then it is ready to paint.

For a still life she uses a lot of muted browns, yellows and other warm tones. Many of her compositions include glass and reflective metals which give little sparkles and highlights. Because of this she uses a dark, matt background, which pushes the objects forward and intensifies the colours. Three layers go into the background — a wash first, and two more layers on top. It is usually a mixture of Lamp Black and Vandyke Brown — black on its own would be far too harsh.

Elaine prefers paints that have become hard in the tube; she says when she buys it the paint is much too soft and tacky and sticks on the brush. Consequently her tubes last her for years and years. To start the

1
Elaine starts by sketching the still life in pencil, only transferring this to the vellum when she is satisfied that all the information is correct. She then applies a wash to the surface to take away its starkness and give her a tonal base to work on.

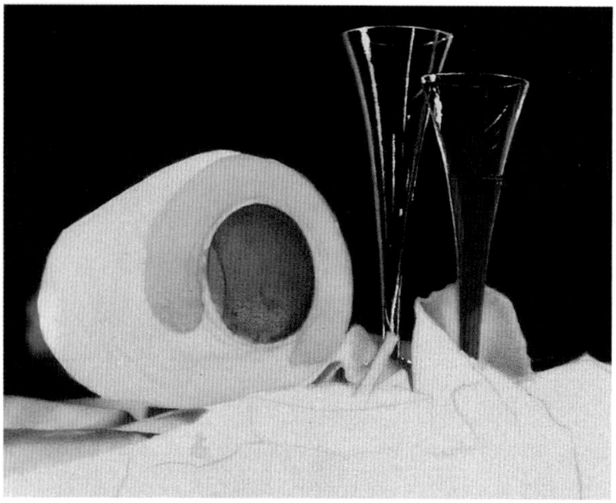

2
Elaine works from the back forwards, always completing one section or item before moving on to the next.

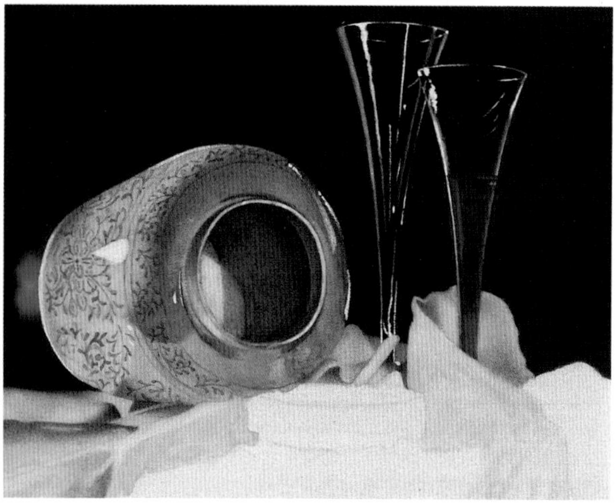

3
The dark, matt background serves to intensify the surfaces and textures in the still life, while the highlights breathe life into the various forms, giving them an almost photographic reality.

Enlargement: To paint something really fine and smooth, such as the reflections on a glass, Elaine uses a magnifying glass. Notice how she has stippled fine details with tiny dots of paint.
Actual size 5.2 x 6.4 cm (2 x 2½ in)

painting, she mixes up the basic colour of the subject and puts in a wash over that area to take away the starkness of the vellum. She will then begin to put on the detail. She works from the farthest point at the back and builds forward, so that she is always painting in the front of the section she has just completed. She tackles the whole painting in sections dictated by the items in the composition. She always completes the object she is painting before moving on to the next. She prefers her frames to pass unnoticed rather than attract attention away from the most important thing — the painting.

When asked what she would say to someone wanting to do similar work Elaine's main advice would be not to be frightened of it. 'If you are at all intimidated by it the end result won't be worth looking at. If it all goes wrong it doesn't matter; don't be daunted by that blank piece of vellum waiting to be filled. Work to your own pace and in your own way, never mind how long anyone else may take, it is each to his own.'

Pauline Gyles
Watercolour on Ivorine

Paints
(usual palette)
Cobalt Blue
French Ultramarine
Cerulean Blue
Yellow Ochre
Raw Sienna
Burnt Umber
Light Red
Violet Mauve
Indian Red
Warm Sepia
Cadmium Red
Cadmium Yellow
Aureolin
Viridian

Base
Ivorine

Brushes
Winsor & Newton,
series 12 and 7,
sizes 1 and 0.

Other materials
Sellotape
Cottonwool
Talcum powder
Tissues
Sharp blade

Pauline Gyles is an award winning portrait artist as well a skilled still life artist. Her still lifes are made up from the everyday things around her, anything that strikes her as an interesting group of colours or shapes. Sometimes the arrangement can seem to start rather haphazardly — she groups together objects that catch her attention, begins painting and will then add another item to balance or complement the rest. She thinks nothing of washing an object out completely if it does not satisfy her. This attitude of letting the painting develop as it is painted gives her work a unique quality and character.

She paints sitting at a table, using a drawing board that is almost vertical. The light from a window comes in at shoulder height on her left and there is a glazed roof over the bay window, so she has plenty of north light, which is ideal. However, she is equally happy painting on a small board balanced on her knee if the still life is set up somewhere awkward.

Left
Jemima, by Pauline Gyles.
Actual size
Pauline's still life work has tremendous charm and atmosphere.

Right
Detail showing Pauline's fluid and easy handling of paint. Notice how she lays little delicate strokes side by side, the width of the brush, to create colour effects.

The piece of Ivorine she is going to use is stuck down on to white card or board, with sellotape holding it down each side. Pauline avoids pencil as it can leave marks even after it is erased, and instead draws her composition straight on to the base using a brush loaded with a pale, watered down mix of the colour in the painting. She tends to work outwards from the focal points, putting in the shapes and colours that make up the main lines of the composition. The first brush strokes are allowed to dry then another layer goes over them so that they are blended together, one coat on top of another, until the required intensity of colour is attained. A sharp blade is used very lightly to remove excess paint and rectify mistakes, or to create highlights.

The finished work is framed as simply as possible to suit the painting. Pauline prefers traditional gold ovals for her portraits but she uses conventional mouldings, with a mount under the glass, for other subjects.

1
Pauline paints in the faintest outlines of her forms, using pale tones of the actual colours.

2
Using a size 1 brush she starts strengthening the colours in fairly loose, easy strokes.

3
To build up the forms, Pauline uses little delicate strokes, typical of miniature painting – tiny, elongated dabs of paint, placed side by side. With layer upon layer she gradually builds up the colour.

Right
Colours and shapes are the motivating forces for Pauline Gyles' still life paintings. She opts for Ivorine because she finds it a very tolerant surface to work on; sections of the painting can be wiped off and repainted if required. Pauline thinks nothing of removing objects and changing items around in her paintings until she is completely satisfied with the composition. *Actual size 9.7 x 7.3 cm (3¾ x 3 in)*

Autumn Flowers
by Pamela Davis

Actual size

Flowers

Pamela Davis

Acrylic on Ivorine

Pamela Davis paints larger works as well as miniatures; for the former, she uses any smooth, hard-surfaced board, hot pressed paper or even copper, but for miniatures she normally uses Ivorine. She says some people seem to be afraid of using acrylics but she maintains that with a little practice they would find it a medium they could really enjoy. Acrylics are immensely versatile as they can be applied straight from the tube like oils or thinned down to use as transparent watercolours. There are many thinners and retarders that can be added for different effects if required, but Pamela only uses water to dilute the paints. When acrylics first came on the market the colours were less subtle. 'Now, so long as you know how to mix them to lose that sweetness of man-made colours, the range is as good as any other paint. Reds and yellows added to the greens will achieve the full range needed for leaves and stems of plants.' For the backgrounds of her flower paintings, she takes the colours from the foliage she is painting, but muted down. Her favourite is a mix of Yellow Ochre and Burnt Umber in varying degrees of light and dark which never seems to conflict with any of the other colours in the painting.

The only brush she ever uses is a size 4 sable. This may seem amazing for miniatures but it has a good reservoir and as long as it achieves a good point it can be used for everything, even the fine, detailed work.

Her advice is to spend time assessing the subject. If it is set up too close to you it tends to end up being too large, so keep it at a reasonable distance to start with then bring it closer to attend to the detail later, after the painting has been blocked in. The painting is drawn in using a half-and-half mixture of green and brown paint, kept extremely pale, and by drawing in the subject with a brush. She puts in the background after the blocking-in stage and before working too much on the painting. This allows any alterations to be made should the background creep into the subject and for edges to be painted over at an early stage if slight mistakes occur. Pamela then gets

Paints
(usual palette)
Rowney Liquitex acrylics:
Titanium White
Yellow Ochre
Burnt Sienna
Burnt Umber
Hooker's Green
Ultramarine
Cadmium Yellow Medium
Cadmium Yellow Pale
Cadmium Red
Cadmium Violet

Base
Ivorine

Brushes
Rowney sable, series 43, size 4.

Other materials
Water to dilute

1

The subject is drawn in using a brush and a half-and-half pale mix of green and brown that will be gradually built up to the final stage.

2

The blocking in is done next, establishing the dark tones as soon as possible to give something to work to. When a variety of pale shades of the finished colours are put in Pamela starts to build up the strength of the paint.

3

Next the background goes in. This allows any slips to be corrected at an early stage so the outer edges are accurate and crisp. After that the intensity of colour is gradually built up accentuating the lighter and darker tones.

Enlarged view of finished painting showing the rich colour effects that can be achieved with acrylics.

in the very dark tones to establish something to work to. She says: 'Don't be afraid to make mistakes at this stage as these can always be worked over.' When she has a variety of tones in the underpainting she starts to put in the colour, letting the under-colour show through.

Very near the end she turns her attention to the detail — the pattern on vases or the stamens on flowers. This is done with exquisite control and she prefers to put in the finishing details in daylight. Acrylic is a medium that dries quickly so she can keep working over previous layers without picking up the paint underneath.

The finished painting is finally framed. The Ivorine is held down by a mount and it should be backed with acid-free paper the same size as the painting which is then taped to the mount. Pamela advises: 'Artists should not be afraid to experiment with colours of mounts and the size of frames.' If you are entering work to societies size restrictions must be observed, but for the artist's own purposes much more sympathetic and interesting effects can be achieved.

Christine Hart-Davies
Watercolour on Paper or Vellum

Christine Hart-Davies is a botanical artist first and foremost. Her paintings are scientifically correct and she knows the structure and habits of all the plants she draws. Her great emphasis is observation and drawing and she is meticulous throughout. This can give her work a deceptively simple appearance; she can make the study of a single piece of fruit on a plain background breathtaking in its purity and simplicity.

Christine sits at a drawing board that is nearly upright and she likes to set up a small vase of flowers on a box on top of the table she is working at. This brings it to the right height so that she is not looking down on it. If she is painting a sprig of a plant, she will Blu-tack it to the board in front of her or even use some 'oasis' taped to the board to keep it fresh and at the right angle. She works from life whenever possible. If this is impossible because her subjects are halfway up a tree in the jungle,

Paints
(usual palette)
Oxide of Chromium
Sap Green (used with caution – she prefers to mix her greens from blues and yellows)
Burnt Sienna
French Ultramarine
Cobalt Blue
Cerulean
Indigo
Winsor Purple
Winsor Violet
Permanent Mauve
Permanent Rose
Alizarin Crimson
Winsor Red
Vermilion
Cadmium Yellow
Chrome Yellow
Winsor Yellow
Yellow Ochre
Davy's Gray
She also uses Ivory Black, Viridian and Neutral Tint, but very sparingly. She mixes all the browns.

Base
Vellum, or Arches hot-pressed watercolour paper.

Brushes
Winsor & Newton, best sable, series 7, size 1 (her favourite brush as it has a good point and also holds a good reservoir of paint). She occasionally uses a finer brush (000) for minute details.

Left
Pitcher Plant, watercolour on vellum, by Christine Hart-Davies.
Actual size
Christine researches the habits and structures of all the palnts she draws. In her paintings she tries to also show the complete ecology of how and where that plant lives.

she takes photos, collects specimens (if allowable) and does sketches on the spot. Then she comes back to the studio to do the final detailed work. She will use half a dozen photographs for one painting, using different aspects to build up a total knowledge of how the plant is put together. Her ultimate preference is to portray the plant in its natural setting, making it more of a picture than a study; she is fascinated by the relationships between plants and animals in the wild.

Before she starts, the vellum or paper is taped to white or cream card. Vellum, in particular, needs to be firmly held with masking tape at the four corners. She secures a hinged mount which is taped to the lefthand side or top so that it can be flipped over the painting at any time. This gives her a 'window' to check the composition while she is working. If she is using vellum, she dampens a tissue with ox-gall and wipes over the whole area quickly

Other materials
- 3H pencil
- Emery board
- Ox-gall
- Scalpel
- Tissues
- Masking tape
- Blu-tack
- Oasis (flower arrangers' foam)
- Water to dilute

Right
Enlarged section illustrating the meticulous attention to detail when using colours.

and evenly. This makes sure it is clean, removing any powder or greasemarks, and provides a slight 'tooth' to the working surface.

Christine first does a very careful outline drawing on the base. Her aim is maximum accuracy with economy of line: 'It is essential to get the drawing really right because everything is so closely looked at in a miniature.' She keeps the pencil (3H) extremely sharp throughout, renewing the point on an emery board at regular intervals. To get rid of any loose graphite, she wipes the pencil on a tissue after each sanding. She makes sure that everything in the drawing is in perspective, measuring the ellipses of vases each side with a template. It is only then, when the information has all been precisely planned out on the base, that she is ready to start painting.

It is difficult putting a wash on vellum as it has a tendency to mottle, so Christine uses more stippling and hatching to cover the paler areas. If she is working on paper, she dampens a small area with clean water, then picks up the colour she needs and floods it in. This keeps the colour even and stops hard 'tide-lines' forming where the paint meets a dry patch. When this flat wash layer has been done on all the areas large enough to allow this method, she starts to add the intensity of colour. This is done by hatching in with a very dry brush and paint, constantly drying her brush on a tissue as she works. It is a slow process, made up of very fine lines following the line of a petal or stem as far as possible. If any spaces are left in between she will go over it again, filling in the paler areas. If the depth of colour is sufficient but there are still a few blemishes after the paint is dry, she takes a clean, damp brush and washes over it again.

Left
Overgrown Spring Border,
by Christine Hart-Davies.
Actual size
Christine is a botanical artist first and foremost so her paintings of flowers have to be meticulously correct and yet she prefers to place them in their natural settings, dead leaves, caterpillars and all.

Christine does not use black, preferring to mix complementary colours to produce the shadows. For example if she is painting a red flower she will mix a strong green into the red she is working with, for a very dark shade to give depth to petals. She sometimes introduces minute quantities of unexpected colours to shadows, such as violets or deep blues. For the highlights she uses white in some cases, preferably gouache: 'Gouache tends to melt more easily than other types of watercolour and can be softened at the edges for more diffused highlights.' It is preferable to leave the white of the paper to form the highlights but this is not always possible. On vellum the paint can be very carefully scratched away with a sharp scalpel blade but some plants have extremely fine hairs growing on the stems that can only be seen with a magnifying glass. These she prefers to put in with gouache, using a very fine brush. She takes a last look to check there are no pencil marks left or rough edges; if there are, they can be tidied up with a scalpel.

Detail of petals showing how colour has been floated into pre-dampened areas.

Finally there is the decision of how the finished work is to be presented. Christine bonds vellum on to card with Copydex to stop it cockling. She protects the painting with tissue paper and flattens the whole under a pile of heavy books. When dry, she trims it to size and either places it in a frame with a gold rim and convex glass or frames it using conventional moulding, with a mount to keep some space between the painting and the glass. She always uses acid-free board.

Barbara Valentine
Watercolour on Ivorine

Paints
(usual palette)
Artists' quality watercolours:
Cobalt Blue
French Ultramarine
Payne's Gray
Scarlet Lake
Alizarin Crimson
Lemon Yellow
Cadmium Yellow
Yellow Ochre
Burnt Sienna
Burnt Umber
Raw Umber
Sepia
Olive Green
Sap Green
Black is only used for silhouettes and white sometimes for highlights.

Base
Ivorine

Brushes
Da Vinci Maestro, Tobolosky-Kolinsky sable, sizes 000 and 4. She also has a variety of other sizes and makes, such as Winsor & Newton, series 12, sizes 4 and 000.

Other materials
Flour paper
Pencil
Masking tape
Pen and ink
Distilled water

Barbara Valentine is a very inspirational artist and everything she portrays in her paintings has symbolic meaning. Her studio is full of objects — shells, vases, silk shawls and feathers — which she uses to tell the story. She usually places a key somewhere in the painting to symbolize unlocking its secrets. Pyramids mean timelessness, pink flowers mean friendship, two parrots mean relationships and a bird and a cat mean danger. Her compositions are made up from a fourfold content of flow, colour, pattern and meaning. They are lovely to look at and fun to decipher.

'It is very important to have the work on a raised surface, at least 2 inches (50 millimetres) above the desk.' Barbara tries to sit in a comfortable upright position and listens to music as she works.

Left
Still Life in a Niche,
by Barbara Valentine
Actual size

A single object or a theme will start the inspiration. She then arranges some of the pieces she is going to paint on a shelf in front of her. She does many sketches, almost doodling in the shapes until they begin to mould into a good composition. When she is satisfied that she has the essential shapes worked out, she goes over the pencil with fine pen and ink to give it more definition. This inked-in drawing is fixed with masking tape to a piece of white card and then a piece of Ivorine placed over it and taped so nothing will move. The drawing shows through but ultimately it is only a guide; if an insect flies into the studio she may include it in the composition. Eventually a plain piece of paper is placed between the drawing and the Ivorine as her first sketch becomes redundant. She uses the frame or mount in which the finished painting will eventually be presented to check that the vertical lines do not 'wander' and to see how the composition looks as a whole. 'Stopping now and again to sit back and take a longer view is also useful.'

In Barbara's experience the Ivorine needs very little preparation. If there does seem to be some grease on it she will rub it over, very gently, with flour paper. Pumice powder can be used for tougher cleaning or if there is a really bad greasemark, such as a fingerprint, a lithographic, fibre-glass eraser works like magic. Everything is kept scrupulously clean. She always uses distilled water to dilute her paints.

Starting on the painting she outlines the larger areas of shapes with a size 000 brush in the palest Cobalt Blue. Then the subject is blocked in, using the palest colours of the finished piece. After this first application the painting is worked up, gaining precision of line as the colours become deeper. Barbara stresses that this should never be done in a heavy-handed way — the secret of transparent colour is to be patient with the gradual, overall intensity, building up layer by layer and taking paint off again if it becomes too heavy: 'If you cannot see through the paint you have too much on.'

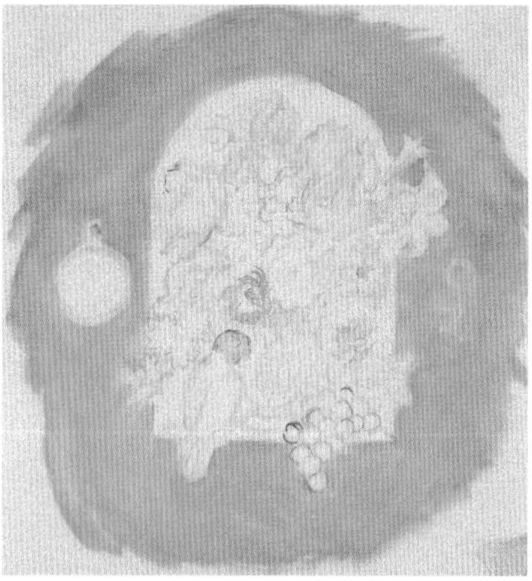

1
Barbara outlines the larger shapes and forms with a size 000 brush using a very pale Cobalt Blue.

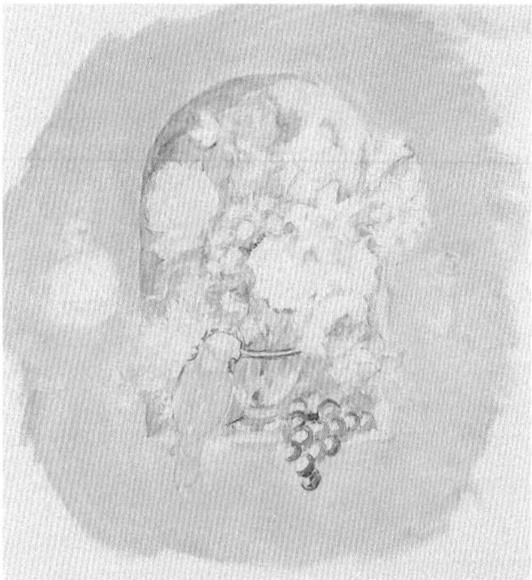

2
The areas are blocked in gradually, using pale versions of their true colours. Some detail starts to be added in. If at any stage Barbara is not happy with the way the painting is going she simply removes the offending area of paint with a wet brush.

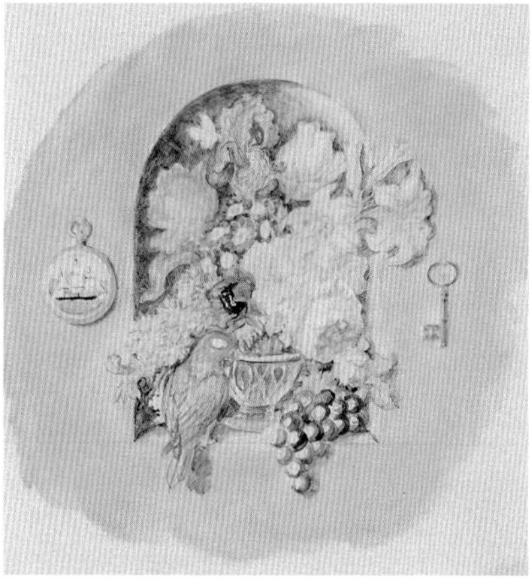

3
The flowers are painted in one at a time, often from sketches. The actual flowers may have long since died before they are immortalised on the Ivorine.

Enlarged view of Still Life in a Niche showing Barbara's controlled application of colour.

Each flower is painted one at a time, either direct from life or from sketches, since flowers can die so fast. A flower still life takes her four or five days without interruptions. Barbara often has two paintings in progress at the same time, so that one can be drying whilst the other is being added to. The finishing touches are put in with drier and drier paint, making for a much crisper sense of detail. She uses the back of a photograph or photographic paper as a palette and to rest her hand on, while tackling the minute detail of the finishing stages.

The Macaw
watercolour on Ivorine
by Joyce Rogerson

Actual size

Animals and Wildlife

Heather O. Catchpole

Watercolour on Ivorine

Heather Catchpole paints human portraits with great success. She also has a great love of animals and her portrayal of dogs reveals her understanding of her subject and her empathy with it.

The dog that is to sit for its portrait visits Heather at her home. She spends time taking it around her garden so that it feels comfortable in her presence. Becoming familiar with the dog's personality is most important and throughout the whole process Heather is getting to know the animal and watching for particular aspects of its character. Some dogs are laid back animals with ears down and dreamy eyes, others are more alert and restless, with ears up, and bright eyes. She takes lots of photographs and makes colour notes: 'Pictures should always be taken at eye level with the dog.' However, you cannot rely on just photographs. Once she had two Springer spaniels visit in the same week and the films were developed at the same time. The dogs were almost identical but their characters were totally different. Heather's whole approach to the portraits differed for each dog so that she tackled the compositions and even the backgrounds differently, according to the nature of each dog.

When she starts the work, Heather collects her notes of the colour details (eyes, hair tones and so on), pencil sketches and photographs taken from many different angles, so that she has as much information as possible. 'The time spent photographing the sitter is most valuable because you are not only recording basic information but registering their character and movements, subconsciously getting to know them.'

Gillie, by Heather Catchpole.
Actual size

Paints
(usual palette)
Winsor & Newton and Schmincke artists' quality watercolours, in half-pans:
Payne's Gray
Yellow Ochre
Light Red
New Gamboge
Raw Sienna
Scarlet Lake
Burnt Sienna
Warm Sienna
French Ultramarine
Cerulean Blue
Burnt Umber
Lamp Black
Gouache, both black and white, is also used occasionally.
She duplicates almost all her colours in both makes; one of her favourite colours, Payne's Gray, illustrates that they are completely different greys. She does not recommend Olive Green, Sap Green, Lemon Yellow and the madders for use on Ivorine.

Base
Ivorine

1
Heather begins this painting of 'Thief' by putting in a pale wash (the basic colour of the fur), and omitting areas where there are light coloured markings.

2
In the early stages she builds up pale washes and then starts to add in shadows to give a sense of the form. She paints the eyes early on since it is these that give the dog its individual character.

3
Once the first layers are dry Heather starts to paint in more detail and strength of colour. The paint is drier for this and the brush strokes follow the growth of the hair.

4
Dogs' noses can be pinky brown or sometimes bluey black. They have to show texture so this area is delicately dotted in. Whiskers are painted with a fine brush but they can also be scratched in with a needle. This finished painting of Thief is shown in its actual size.

Heather takes the frame that she plans to use and, laying it on a piece of paper, draws a line round the inside to give her the exact picture size. This is placed under the layout paper she does the initial drawing on, as a template for the finished size. Using a 2B pencil, she draws sketch after sketch until she has achieved the likeness she knows is right. The square or oval acts as her guide under each attempt, so there is no need for scaling up or down when she decides on the one she will use. She then uses a lightbox, placing the clean Ivorine base over her drawing, with the light shining through. This enables her to 'draw' in the fine outline, using a soft, warm grey paint on the brush. She says: 'You must always be careful where the picture is placed on the piece of Ivorine, allowing a good 1/2 inch (12·5 mm) border which gives room to manoeuvre and the chance to make the picture slightly larger if need be.'

To paint the portrait of a dog she puts in a pale wash similar to the basic colour of the fur. The first stages are done by layering pale washes: 'It is most important to get the tones right before the hair is worked up.' Then she starts building up the shadows to indicate the form. The eyes are put in at a very early stage — the personal contact and character come from the eyes and she likes to establish that as soon as possible. She paints in the dark colour of the eyes and lifts out the paint for the light parts: 'Always remember that the iris of the eye is lighter on the dark side of the face, which is the opposite from what you would expect.' She puts in a tiny dot of gouache white to bring the eye to life.

Once the first layers are dry she starts to paint in more detail and strength of colour. The paint is drier for this and the brush strokes follow the growth of the hair. The technique is finer in a miniature and the tones are built up with the brush as the painting progresses.

When the painting is finished information about the sitter, such as name, date, place of birth and so on is noted and put inside the frame.

BRUSHES

Kolinsky sable, short bristled: Winsor & Newton, series 12, sizes 0, 1 and 2.
Pro Arte, series 2A, sizes 00 and 000.
Rowney, series 46, size 2.
Cornelissen, sable spotter.

OTHER MATERIALS

2B pencils
Layout paper
Lightbox
Tweezers
Putty eraser

Sylvia Cave
WATERCOLOUR ON VELLUM

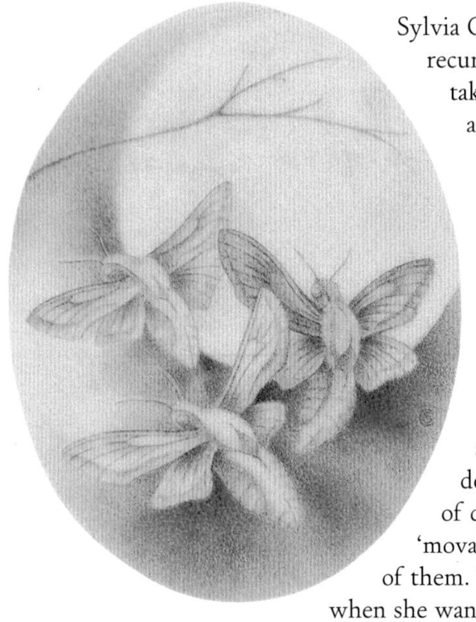

Sylvia Cave is fascinated by the recurring patterns in nature and takes a special interest in insects and reptiles, which she says have a jewel like quality. She certainly achieves some very interesting and beautiful paintings with unusual subject matter.

The first steps are studies and sketches. Her ideas and inspiration come initially from observation of plants, animals and insects. Then she does a series of sketches out of doors, bringing back the more 'movable' items and making studies of them. These stand her in good stead when she wants to incorporate something in a composition that is out of season. Sometimes she catches insects and keeps them for a short time, letting them go again when she has studied them. She makes colour notes and when painting always works either with the subject or the studies. Photographs of creatures that will not keep still long are useful for reference. She never kills anything but if people find dead animals and bring them to her she will use them to learn from, sometimes keeping them in the freezer for a while.

'Then,' she says, 'it is really a question of what format you are going to use.' She tends to decide from the beginning what size the picture is going to be, particularly for miniatures. She likes to find the edges at an early stage and to relate the composition to them. If it is to be round or oval, this can make quite a difference. She finds this a most interesting exercise that is very much part of her construction of ideas. She likes to start free and to capture the movement, building up to the detail. The structure is worked out through drawings on tracing

PAINTS
(usual palette)
Artists' quality watercolours, in tubes (she finds these give more variability of texture and are kinder to the brush):
Cadmium Yellow
Cadmium Lemon
Lemon Yellow Hue
Cadmium Red
Permanent Magenta (Quinacridone) ('a lovely lightfast colour'),
Permanent Rose,
Antwerp Blue (one of her favourites)
Cobalt Blue (often mixed with a little French Ultramarine to give it carrying power and 'spark it up')
Cerulean Blue
Zinc White gouache
Occasionally Permanent White gouache

BASE
Manuscript vellum, no. 1 finish (not treated with pumice).

BRUSHES
Winsor & Newton, series 12 and series 7, sizes 000-1.

Left
Moths and the Moon,
by Sylvia Cave. *Actual size*
Sylvia likes to work with a limited palette and here shows her fascination with the translucent quality of moths' wings.

paper, although she warns that if you plan it out in too much detail it can lose its vitality. She likes to place her work on an easel to allow her to stand back and make sure the design reads well even from a distance. 'The preparatory work, the drawing and the design and all the thought and planning sometimes make the painting seem almost irrelevant. At least you are on the home stretch by then.'

The main elements are transferred on to the vellum by reversing the tracing paper and drawing over the lines on the back with an HB pencil, then pressing through with a 2H pencil. It is important not to press too hard or you can score the vellum. She likes her pencils extremely sharp and uses a scalpel blade to keep them so. The line ends up almost like a dust on the vellum, and can be brushed off with a paintbrush if required or lifted off delicately with a plastic eraser. This means you can still change things if you want. A curve or line can start to evolve and may inspire a slight change to the original idea. It is a strange combination of control and, at the same time, freedom to exploit the interesting concepts that occur.

To prepare the vellum she tips a little pumice powder on the surface and brushes it around to absorb any grease. The powder must all be removed by turning the vellum upside down and giving it a little tap if necessary. There is a hair and a flesh side to vellum — the flesh side is smoother and slightly greasier, but the hair side is the better to paint on. The piece of vellum is then taped by the corners on to a white background.

OTHER MATERIALS
- Tracing paper
- HB and 2H pencils
- Scalpel
- Plastic eraser
- Pumice powder
- Ox-gall
- Hand held magnifying glass.
- Two pots of water, one to dilute and one for washing brushes.

The Garden Pond, by Sylvia Cave. *Actual size*

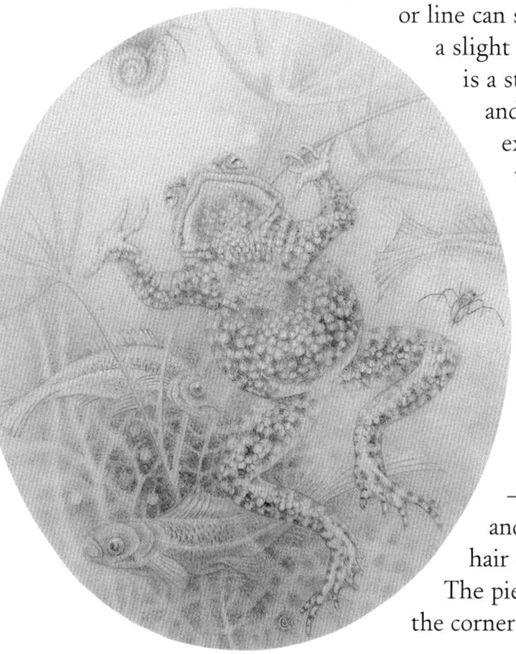

A mount is placed over it, for two reasons: to prevent touching the vellum with your hands and to provide the edges. If possible, it is a good idea to have a mount of the colour you are going to finally use for framing because you will paint to that colour tone; even off-whites can vary a lot.

1

Sylvia works out all the colours to be included before she starts painting. She prefers a very limited palette, especially for miniatures. She mixes all her secondaries and neutrals but she finds earth colours do not work well for her on vellum — they seem too 'thick or gooey'. She prefers to make up the darker colours for shadows from complementary colours she is using; to suddenly introduce something different would spoil the harmony and coherence in her opinion. Very occasionally she uses a drop of ox-gall in the water if she finds the paint is not free-flowing enough.

2

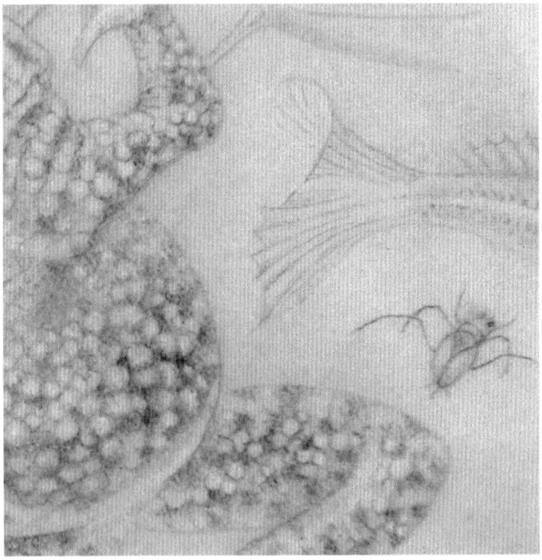

She paints sitting at a table with a drawing board set at a sloping angle. She uses a hand-held magnifying glass, which she prefers to keep adjusting and could not work with fixed. She always has two pots of water as cleanliness is vital for clear clean colour.

To start, she lightly puts in the basic colouring. It is terribly important to note where the light and dark areas are going to be. Once the under-painting has provided her colour balance, she turns her attention to the dominant features. The delicate parts or background areas should not become too strong too quickly or they will unbalance the

3

1
Detail of The Garden Pond

2
Detail of The Garden Pond

3
Detail of The Garden Pond

From these three enlarged views you can see the pleasure Sylvia takes in the patterns she finds in nature, both on the toad and in the delicately intertwined reeds.

rest, so they are left, to return to later. The gold of the toad illustrated here is painted in very much brighter to start with, almost too bright and sugary; it can be dulled back later to a more realistic colour but it is very much harder to liven it up from the dull tones. The under-painting gives everything a glow. She uses white gouache on occasion although the glow of the vellum is usually enough. If she does use white it can help to give a textured feel, for example on the skin of the toad. When the basic structure of the amphibian (or reptile) is safely established, the next stage is to start putting in the detail of the skin. All the scales, warts and little bumps, as well as the local colour markings, are built up by highlights. She has worked out the detail of every feature in the preparatory drawing so this stays placed beside her for reference. Then she returns to working up the background.

Sylvia has experimented with using silk as a base for miniatures because it gives such a beautiful natural sheen and translucent sparkle, ideal for some of her watery subjects. She has managed to use her normal paints, without bleeding, by keeping them at just the right dryness: 'There is an absolute lack of resistance and the slightest touch registers which, whilst exciting, can also have its disadvantages.' She is still working on scaling the technique down in a controlled enough manner for good miniature work.

Finally the painting is taped along one edge to attach it to acid-free board. This allows it to move, something vellum is very prone to. The mount, also cut from acid-free board, prevents it from touching the glass or the frame and holds it in place.

Kathleen Nelson

Watercolour or Oil on Vellum or Lumitex

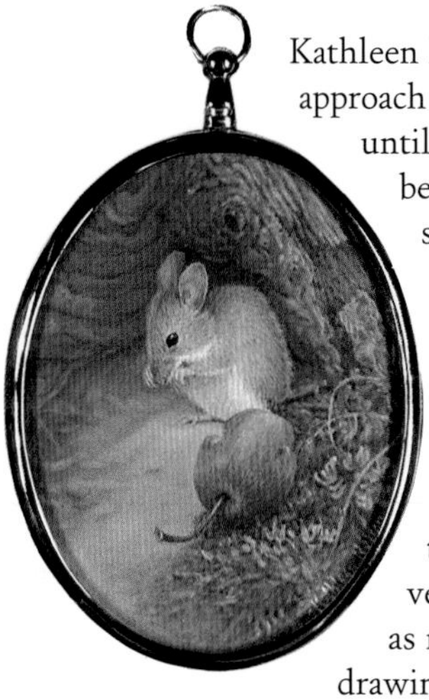

Kathleen Nelson's paintings are as delicate as her approach to the wild animals she studies, watching until she has absorbed every detail of their behaviour and character. She sits out in the snow drawing frost and all the things you cannot bring into the house. She says she is not a very good photographer but instead she has sketchbooks full of studies of mice, birds, tree roots and many plants and animals. These detailed drawings are used to provide a tracing of lines to put the shape of the composition on to the vellum. It almost seems a waste to spend as much time and trouble as she does on a drawing, working it up until it is beautiful enough to be a completed work in its own right, but the process is all important to her. By taking so much care she learns how the animal moves and what attitudes it will take up. Kathleen has even kept small animals such as mice and rabbits and she is now so familiar with some of them the likeness achieved is almost instinctive. If she is watching a wildlife programme on television she is able to do a rough drawing of the animals she is familiar with during the short time they are on the screen. When she starts painting, most of the work goes in freehand and she can refer to the drawing if she needs to.

When Kathleen is using oils she paints straight on to the vellum as it has quite a good surface. For glazes she adds oil painting medium but otherwise she thins the paint with pure turpentine. She cuts in the main blocks of colour very loosely just to cover it all. Then she lets that dry before going on to the next stage. From then on she begins to work up the colours and textures. If a mistake is made, it is still quite easy to wipe it off at this stage so long as the colour underneath has been allowed to dry properly: 'If the design has been worked out well beforehand there shouldn't be any mistakes. It has been fixed in your head.'

Paints

(usual palette)
Oil paints:
Titanium White
Cadmium Yellow
Cadmium Lemon
Yellow Ochre
Cadmium Red
Alizarin Crimson
Light Red
Burnt Umber
Burnt Sienna
Cerulean Blue
Cobalt Blue
French Ultramarine
Permanent Green Light
Viridian
Ivory Black
Some of her 37ml tubes are 20 years old, they last such a long time; small tubes would be much more convenient.

Base

Vellum (Kelmscott) or Lumitex

Left
Woodmouse and Crab-apple,
by Kathleen Nelson. *Actual size*

Below
Kathleen's sketchbook studies of birds.

After the first stage is dry Kathleen relies far less on turpentine to thin the paint. She prefers to use the artists' painting medium as it improves the gloss of the paint and keeps it more transparent. It also seems to mix much better — she puts a spot of medium on the palette and then mixes the colour in. It is best not to get the paint too thick. Towards the end she is trying to keep the paint for the shadows as thin as possible, building up with transparent layers of clear colour rather than using any white which would make it opaque. When it comes to rougher textures such as the bark of a tree or moss for instance, then she would include white and use thicker paint, finally glazing over even that.

Kathleen tends to use more glazes in the final stages, which means giving the paint time to dry between each application. This could take a day or two, depending on how thin the layers are.

BRUSHES
For watercolours: Winsor & Newton, series 12, size 4 (for blocking in, where it is more a case of getting the paint on rather than using fine strokes); Rowney, series 34, sizes 00-4; Winsor & Newton sable, series 7, size 1 and sometimes uses 000 for whiskers.
For oils: Prolene, Pro Arte 101.
The make and size do not matter as much as getting a good brush with a fine point: 'They just get nice to work with and then they die.'

OTHER MATERIALS
Ox-gall (for watercolours).
Winsor & Newton artists' oil painting medium.
Turpentine (for oils)

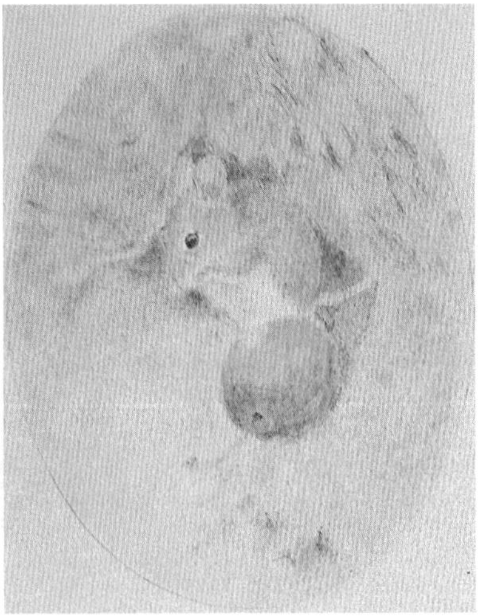

1
The composition is blocked in using oil paint thinned with turpentine straight on to the vellum. This should be left to dry before going on to the next stage.

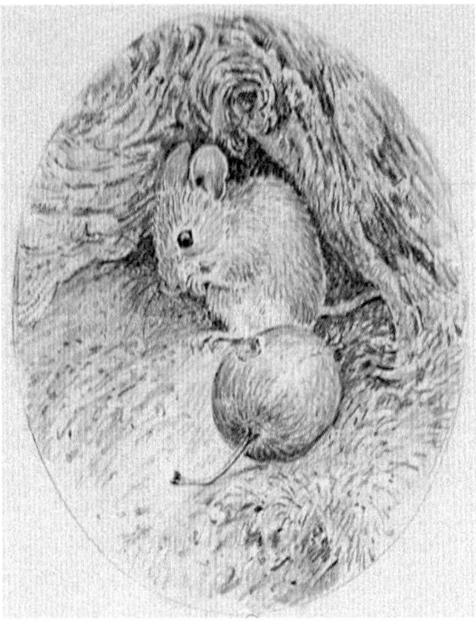

2
The work is then built up in both colour and texture. The paint is now thinned with artists' painting medium. Shadows should be put in with layer on layer of thin transparent colour, whilst logs, for instance, would have opaque white used so the paint is put on a little thicker and allows texture.

3
The final colours are built up of thin glazes. These must be left to dry between layers and patience is needed not to build too quickly, even if the whole process takes several days.

Finished work, greatly enlarged.

Joyce Rogerson
WATERCOLOUR ON IVORINE

Joyce Rogerson paints some delightful miniatures of birds, butterflies, animals and flowers, usually in their natural surroundings. She takes her subjects from life studies as far as possible, collecting feathers, etc., but it is not really advisable to ask what she has in her freezer! Friends bring her dead animals they have found and she has had one or two stuffed to use for reference, but she prefers to see them alive. She does sketches, takes many photographs and observes — many of her subjects live in her back garden. Joyce now has a stock of sketches for when flowers are not in season and these can be scaled down for a miniature.

She paints sitting at an upright board, with the painting pinned to polystyrene and a piece of kitchen paper under her hand. Although she has a magnifying glass with a daylight bulb incorporated underneath, she seems to use it mainly for the light it gives. Instead she has devised an ingenious way of wearing a plastic sun visor with a double magnifier clipped to the front, which gives her 3x magnification. She paints looking through this but if she wants to look long distance she can lift it and she can see her paints by glancing to the side.

When Joyce is using Ivorine she cuts it to size by placing the glass from the frame she intends to use over it and marking round it. The glass in some frames can be

PAINTS
(usual palette)
Mostly Winsor & Newton plus some Rowney artists' quality watercolours, in tubes:
Sap Green
Hooker's Green
Cadmium Red
Cadmium Yellow
Raw Sienna
Burnt Sienna
Yellow Ochre
Winsor Green
Sepia
Burnt Umber
Magenta
Alizarin Crimson
French Ultramarine
Payne's Gray
Manganese Blue
Cobalt Violet
Gouache:
Spectrum Violet
Flame Red
Chinese Orange
Cadmium Primrose
Permanent White

BASE
Ivorine or vellum

BRUSHES
Winsor & Newton, series 12, sizes 000 and 00. She also likes a size 4 Rekab from Simonart, a Kolinsky sable which is resilient, has good spring and a perfect point.

Left
The Macaw, by Joyce Rogerson.
Actual size
Joyce normally paints over all areas of the work, not concentrating on any particular part. Here she painted the bird last.

smaller than it should be and the edge of the Ivorine would show, as well as leaving it loose in the frame, so it is advisable to check that it is a good fit before you start painting. She makes sure the surface is completely clean by washing it in detergent and rinsing it well. Once this has been done, she tries to avoid touching the surface, holding the Ivorine only at the edges, because even a little grease may stop the paint from 'taking'.

Joyce makes a drawing to size, working out the proportions and deciding where everything is to be. This is copied on to the Ivorine by 'drawing' it on in a pale French Ultramarine wash, just to get the right perspective for the creature but not to put in the background. If she is using vellum, she draws with a 0.3 mm lead pencil, taking it off by dabbing gently with a putty eraser if it becomes at all heavy. The vellum is stuck on to card with gum arabic and pressed flat until it is quite secure. She then proceeds to block in with almost a wash of colour, paler but of the same hue as the final painting. This part is tricky as the paint must be of the right consistency. On either base, the paint must be used fairly dry because if it is too wet it will tend to buckle the vellum or else roll off the Ivorine:

'The paint should always be applied delicately. Don't start off by putting it on too thickly; use small quantities but fairly dry. Stippling gives the best control when you come to achieve a depth of colour.'

She has recently started putting a couple of drops of gum-arabic in the water. She tries not to use too much white until almost the end and only for highlights.

Other materials
Gum Arabic
Kitchen paper
Plastic sun visor with double magnifiers (x 3).
3mm lead pencil
Putty eraser
Water to dilute

Enlargement showing the attention to detail and the intricate use of pattern in the plumage.

Square Riggers
by Cdr. G. W. G. Hunt

Actual size

Seascapes

Cdr. G. W. G. Hunt

Acrylic on Board

Geoff Hunt is a retired Royal Navy Commander and knows his subject extremely well. Not only is he exceptionally good at painting the sea, he gets the technicalities right too.

He often paints on wood or similar surfaces, for example the lids of antique snuffboxes, as well as using hardboard for a picture that is to be framed. The hardboard is cut to size beforehand and the smooth side is rubbed with a fine abrasive paper to roughen it evenly all over. Watered down gesso is applied initially and left to really soak in and then dry for about half an hour. A second coat is applied with a nylon brush, stiff enough to spread it evenly without streaking. This can be rubbed down again if there are any marks. It is very important to have a good painting surface to start with as any ridges or bumps will show through all the subsequent layers and will interfere with the final painting, since anything out of place is noticed at this scale.

If Geoff is painting a period picture — a famous battle scene with sailing ships, for instance — he will research all the individual ships, the disposition of the contestants and the weather conditions. Then he makes a series of sketches, considering what will make the best composition and be an attractive painting. In his paintings of modern battleships, he likes to put a lot of action and movement into the picture, using plumes of water from shellbursts to concentrate the attention and keep the eye focused on the story he wants to convey. Ships must have room to manoeuvre, otherwise the whole scene loses credibility. All this is worked out in pencil, together with the tonal values, in a sketch he will refer to throughout the painting. Then he makes a basic outline drawing on the pre-primed board, in pencil.

The first paint is applied fairly loosely, putting in the sky, sea, ships and any other important features. There are about five stages but basically he is building up the information with more and more contrast and detail all the time, sitting back now and again to check that the light and dark tones are balanced and that there is not too much build-up of colour where it is not wanted.

Paints
(usual palette)
Acrylics:
French Ultramarine
Payne's Gray
Burnt Umber
Burnt Sienna
Hooker's Green
Titanium White
He never uses black, but often mixes Burnt Umber and French Ultramarine for dark shades.

Base
Standard piece of hardboard (smooth side), primed with gesso primer. (He also uses Ivorine).

Brushes
Sable, sizes 000-3.
Nylon brushes for priming, etc.

Other materials
Gesso primer
Kitchen paper
Cottonwool buds
Pencil
Magnifiers (x3), worn on the head.
Spray varnish

1
The first paint is applied fairly loosely, putting in the sky, sea, ships and any other important features. The information is built up by gradually adding more and more contrast and detail.

2
To create the sense of movement in the sea, it must be carefully but freely painted; if it is too meticulous, it loses life. Geoff adds the spray by spattering a mixture of Titanium White and a little Ultramarine on to the surface, flicking the paint off an old round nylon brush. Any paint that lands where it is not required is removed straight away with a cottonwool bud. For the glint on the water he mixes a thick blend of Ultramarine, Hooker's Green and Titanium White and with a pen knife he scrapes it over lightly and quickly where he wants it, giving a sparkle to the waves.

3
To catch the glint of sunlight on the rigging Geoff uses a very fine brush with a good point. He loads this with a mix of Titanium White and Raw Sienna until the paint is almost strung out beyond the point of the brush. Poising it where he wants to start, he drags it swiftly and skilfully across his image, drawing an extraordinarily fine line of bright reflection.

Final stage: Seascapes that include ships need not only the ability of bringing the water to life but the technical knowledge to depict the sails and the flags flying in the right direction with the wind.

Geoff paints the sea fairly loosely and freely, so that it has a sense of movement. He adds the spray by flicking paint off the end of an old brush and creates the sense of shine in the water by a technique involving drawing a pen knife across the paint. To catch the glint of sunlight on details such as the rigging he takes a fine brush loaded with Titanium White and Raw Sienna and drags it quickly and firmly in the direction he wants, creating the thinnest possible line of bright reflection. These techniques take confidence and practice but they illustrate that there are many ways of painting boldly even within the confines of a miniature.

When finished, the painting is checked for any specks of dust or tiny fibres. These can be removed with care, using a sharp knife. If the worst happens and a tiny blob of paint comes away, this can still be put right.

The paint must be thoroughly dry before the varnish is applied. Geoff has tried many ways of doing this but now favours spray as the best method of coating evenly. However, the pressure may drop as the can empties, causing mottling; he never uses a can that is much less than half full. The varnish must not be streaky and it must not 'puddle'. Again, this is where the confidence of experience is useful. It should be done quickly, lightly and evenly.

Flagged Interior with Bluebells
by Elisabeth Lake

Actual size

Interiors

Elisabeth Lake

Watercolour on Ivorex

Elisabeth Lake cannot go anywhere that she appreciates without wanting to record it. She is moved by atmosphere and light; a place doesn't have to be old for her to love it, but it must have character. When she started painting she was fascinated by Beatrix Potter's work and studied her paintings in depth. She learnt a great deal about colour from them although now she has adapted and perfected her own style, evolving into miniatures.

She takes photographs and makes sketches. When she is somewhere that attracts her she tries to get down as much information as possible, making notes all over her sketches about light, colours and details to remind her when she gets home. She says it is impossible to do miniatures away from the studio.

Elisabeth lives in a small country cottage with as much character as she could wish for, reminiscent of her paintings. She paints sitting at the kitchen table with the warmth of the stove behind her. The work is flat and she has the light from an adjustable table lamp. All her references are spread around on the table as she starts the drawing which will form the basis of the final painting. Often this drawing is not of miniature size, so it has to be reduced to be lightly transferred on to the Ivorex. She used to square everything down in scale by the grid method but has recently started photocopying her original to reduce it. This is then traced on to the base, using as few lines as possible to give her a workable outline: 'It is possible to rub out but you must never put it on hard in the first place. To remove it can irritate the surface and it is never right again if that happens.'

The whole painting is blocked in with a first layer of Yellow Ochre. The lightest parts are left, making the most of the light from the start. The second layer is usually Cerulean, with a warmer red forming the third layer; details and highlights of colour are put in last. Ivorex is basically non-porous as long as the paints are kept fairly dry. Elisabeth always hatches rather than stippling, preferring tiny lines to dots. She says: 'You have to follow

Paints
(usual palette)
Various makes of artists' quality watercolours:
Ultramarine (for mixing with browns)
Cobalt Blue
Cerulean
Winsor Violet
Davy's Grey
Yellow Ochre
Raw Umber
Sepia
Vandyke Brown
Raw Sienna
She has Lemon Yellow, a lighter blue and Vermilion for specific work (eg painting holly berries). She mixes all her greens.

Base
Ivorex

Brushes
Winsor & Newton, series 12, size 000.
She loves the elegant handles on Isabey brushes and saves one in perfect condition to do her signature.

Other materials
Water to dilute

1
Elisabeth works in three layers of colour, almost like photographic plates. She is fascinated by tone and is experienced enough to know how each strength of a colour will respond when a layer of a second colour is added on top. First the painting is blocked in in Yellow Ochre, with areas of Ivorex left unpainted for eventual highlight.

2
The second layer is Cerulean. Notice how this affects and transforms the yellow.

3
The final layer is red, giving a warm tone to the overall painting. Elisabeth adds the details at the end, applying the paint in tiny lines of colour.

the form or it goes against the grain.' She does not work in sections, maintaining it must be a harmonious whole: 'If something jumps out at you, it is probably wrong. Watercolours have a way of settling back into the paper. When the painting is left overnight, try to look at it the next morning as though you have never seen it before. Turning it upside down also gives you a different angle or fresh view of it.'

She has a unique way of handling stones (and moss) which gives them a mass and texture which is fascinating. Her flagstones are painted first in an opaque ochre, with layers of reddish purple on top to make it really dark. She starts taking the colour back again, cooling it down with more Yellow Ochre and Davy's Grey and ending up with cool, pale milky blue and perhaps some pale lemon where the light from a door or window shines through. The effect is wonderful and somehow the flagstones also convey mass and weight.

Detail showing Elisabeth's technique of hatching colour.

Wuthering Heights
gouache on parchment
by Christopher Hope-King

Actual size

Illustration

Christopher Hope-King
Watercolour on Bristol Board and Parchment

Christopher Hope-King likes to make us smile with his quirky portraits of famous characters depicted as ducks. He says his portraits evoke strong reactions — people either like them or loathe them. Some people find them surreal or even sinister.

He prefers traditional materials. The parchment he uses is secondhand having previously been used for legal documents. He sings the praises of Bristol board: 'You can block in and lift off paint beautifully to get shading. This is not as successful with paper, which absorbs the colour. The surface of the board can be worked over quite a few times and still remain smooth. It is not the end of the world if you make a mistake.'

He has a good studio but paints sitting in a comfortable chair, using a board resting on his knee. He uses a hand-held magnifying glass for the extremely detailed work.

To start, he marks out the size of the frame then draws within these lines, directly on to the base, using an HB

Paints
(usual palette)
Winsor & Newton artists' quality watercolours in half pans:
French Ultramarine
Crimson Lake
Cadmium Red
Cadmium Yellow Deep
White designers' gouache.
He makes black by mixing everything together.

Base
Bristol board
or parchment

Brushes
Winsor & Newton
series 12, size 000

Other materials
HB pencil
Acrylic Gesso Primer
Gold leaf (on tissue paper).
Rowney gold size for raised borders.
Hand-held magnifying glass.

Detail showing Christopher's delight in putting a miniature painting within his miniature illustration.

1

2

3

4

The Earl of Essex, by Christopher Hope-King. Christopher likes to depict famous figures as ducks. He uses rich colours and borders decorated with gold leaf. *Illustration size 7.5 x 6.5 cm (3 x 21/2 in).*

1
Christopher starts by carefully working out the design in pencil. This is the time to adjust any errors of perspective.

2
He blocks in the drawing with a pale wash. When every part is noted in paint, he rubs out the pencil lines.

3
The colour is stippled on in sections, starting with the floor.

4
The blue background and highlights are added last. White designer's gouache is added for the highlights. Soft contours are created by lifting colour off with a clean brush.

pencil in the most minimal way just to achieve the outline. He says he is not good at drawing so keeps it loose, nevertheless he achieves great precision of line and the composition is very carefully worked out. Perspective is one of his strong points.

He then lays on a pale wash to block in the drawing. When every part is noted in paint, he rubs out the pencil marks. From then on he uses stippling to put in all the colour, maintaining it gives the best control. He even stipples in entire background areas, using a size 000 brush for the whole painting.

Christopher makes a point of tackling the most difficult part of the painting first. He feels that if he has spent ten days or two weeks on a piece, it is not worth the risk of making a mistake and ruining the whole thing at the last minute. He then builds up the sections, still by stippling, until he has an overall strength of colour and texture. His colours, though rich, are mainly opaque. Where a strong highlight is needed, he uses white in the form of designers' gouache; he also makes maximum use of the possibilities of lifting colour off with a clean brush to create soft contours and shapes. All his colours are mixed from the four listed.

To frame his miniatures, he follows tradition and uses a gold square or oval with a ring at the top and convex glass. This adds contrast to the slightly offbeat subject and seems exactly right.

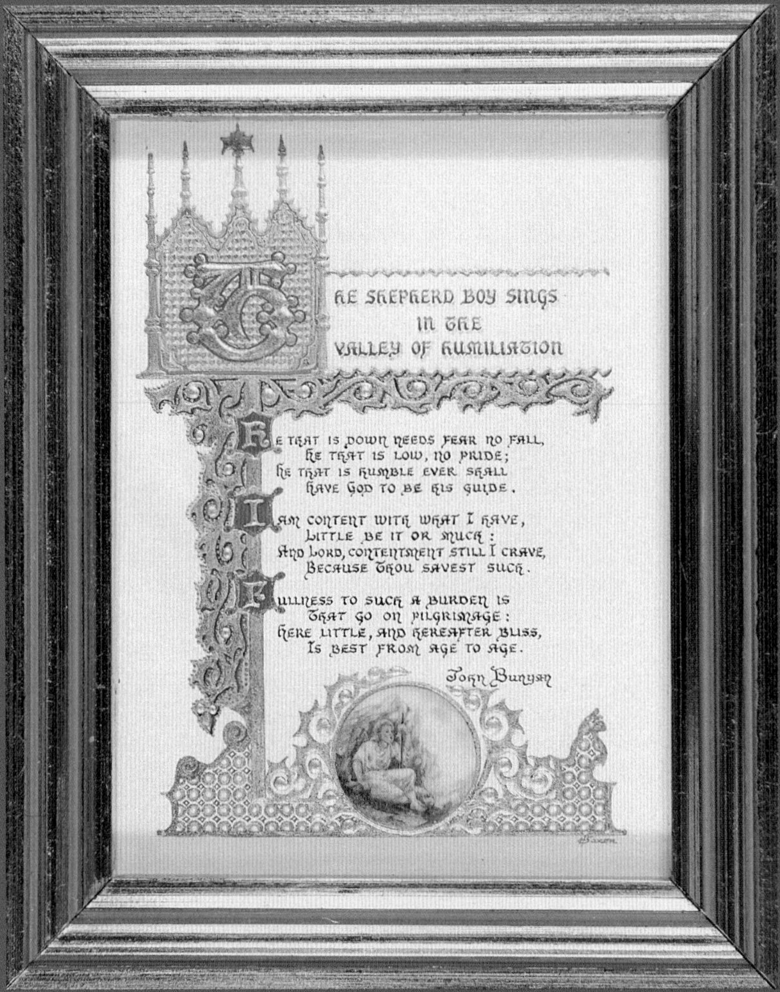

'The Shepherd Boy Sings...'
watercolour on Bristol board
by Henry Saxon

Actual size

Illumination

Henry Saxon

Watercolour on Vellum and Bristol Board

Paints
(usual palette)
Black Rotring drawing ink. Winsor & Newton artists' quality watercolours:
French Ultramarine
Alizarin
Viridian
Winsor Emerald
Cadmium Red
Gamboge
Yellow Ochre
White gouache

Base
Vellum or Bristol board. (Ivorine is sometimes used for small paintings incorporated in the design.)

Brushes
Winsor & Newton, series 29, spotting sable, size 00. Mitchell pen nibs, pedigree round hand, No. 6 (adapted).

Henry Saxon's remarkable work could discourage people as it may seem too exacting to emulate, but anyone wanting to try it should give themselves a chance — after all, Henry as been working at it for about fifty years.

Being so precise, he has thought his technique through to the last detail. His pen is made from an ordinary pen handle and nibs; it is the way he prepares them that makes the difference. He wraps and then sticks fine wet-and-dry sanding paper round a piece of dowelling a little bigger than a pencil. This goes into the chuck of a firmly clamped power drill, just as a drill bit would. He then very carefully grinds away the shoulders of the pen nib, bringing the point to the width he requires for fine lettering. Only very gentle pressure is needed, otherwise the two halves of the nib could split or distort.

Henry also built the wooden board on which he supports his work. It measures 610 x 380 millimetres (24 x 15 inches) and is just under 24 millimetres (3/4 inch) thick. It is in two layers, with a circle 150-200 millimetres (6-8 inches) diameter cut out of the centre of the top layer. A pivot is inserted in the exact centre of the cut-out circle so that it can be slotted back in the board and operated like a turntable. Two small metal brackets on each side carry bolts which act as a register, holding everything firmly in position. A magnifying glass attached to a wooden arm is fixed to the left corner of the board so that it pivots like the arm on a record player. His ruler (from a graphics suppliers) slots on to pins in the board, ensuring strictly accurate positioning every time. His set square is designed to overlap the ruler, so that nothing can slip out of position. He says even the width of the margins on the ruler can make a difference, depending whether you measure using the top or bottom of the line.

His inspiration starts with a poem, quotation or piece of scripture. Often people commission him to illustrate a favourite saying. Depending on the length of the writing, he decides the size of the lettering and the space, and whether it is a subject that lends itself to illustration

1
Henry uses a very fine lead in a propelling pencil to draw in the design. Because precision is the key to his work, he constantly sharpens the pencil by rubbing it on very fine sandpaper. The lines have to be faint but exact.

2
The lettering is done first. For this he uses a pen, dropping tiny amounts of ink on to the nib. It is a painstaking matter to draw in each letter, and one he approaches with great care.

3
The next stage is to apply the gold leaf. If any part of the design is to be raised, Henry uses Winsor & Newton raising preparation which he applies with a brush. It can take up to eight hours for this to dry. He uses transfer type gold leaf which he burnishes on to the required sections of his work.

Detail showing enlargement of inset motif.

Other materials
Graphics ruler
Set square
Propelling pencil with a B 0.5 lead, fine emery paper.
Acrylic primer
Gold leaf
Gold size, Winsor & Newton's raising preparation.
Burnishing tool (agate).
Tissues
Tracing paper
Pastel
Needle
Putty eraser
Ox-gall
Wet-and-dry sanding paper.
Wood glue

or to a decorative border. The next consideration is how much gold leaf to include in the decoration – after the lettering the gold leaf is the hardest part. Then the base is secured to the board using double-sided tape.

Once the work has been planned he draws in the guidelines, which have to be perfect from the start or the spacing will be wrong. He uses a very fine lead (B) in a propelling pencil, which he keeps needle sharp by rubbing it on fine emery paper. Even the angle the pen is held at is critical; it must be the same every time or it will alter the spacing. The less graphite put on the vellum the better; the lines should be faint but exact. He always squares up by marking a central line down and across, then counts out the necessary number of lines. It is easy to vary the width by squashing up or lengthening out the letters a little, but you cannot vary the length if there are a set number of lines in a poem.

Henry always does the lettering first. He is endlessly

patient, doing a few letters at a time or at the most one or two words. A lot depends on the temperature: if it is cold the ink does not dry as fast and he can continue a little longer. He drops a tiny amount of ink on to the nib, just below the reservoir; he does not dip the nib into the ink. After every few words, he cleans the nib with water and a damp tissue. He has to be careful not to get the tiniest hair in the nib or it will drag the ink, and if the nib isn't cleaned regularly it can clog. If one letter is out of place or one word misspelt the piece is ruined, so when it is done he asks a reader to check it.

For the next stage, he traces the design on to tracing paper, rubs an appropriate colour pastel on the back and then transfers it by pressing with a needle. If the design is to be repeated on opposite sides, he turns the paper over, as in a mirror image, and repeats it exactly. The pencil lines are rubbed out with a putty eraser or Blu-tack.

The next stage is to apply the gold leaf. If the title letter or any part of the design is to be raised, he uses Winsor & Newton raising preparation applied with a brush. This is allowed to dry which, if it is very thick, can take eight hours or overnight. Then the size is applied to the design, wherever the gold is required to stick and goes over the raising preparation. This is also put on with a brush, as carefully as possible, and is the basis for all the fine lines and curlicues that look like gold filigree work. It needs to dry fairly quickly as there is a danger of it picking up dust or impurities; a hairdrier will speed the process if necessary. If the work has to be left for any length of time, he takes care to cover it. When it is dry he breathes on the work and the condensation of his breath on the size makes the gold leaf adhere to it. Henry uses the transfer type of gold leaf, which is supplied lightly adhering to tissue paper. The sheet of gold leaf is placed over the area required and peeled off, leaving a small amount of gold. This is carefully burnished with a soft handkerchief or a burnishing tool. If any loose bits remain where they are not wanted, they can be gently brushed off with a flat sable brush. Any irregularities on the edges of the gold leaf (which, in Henry's case, need a magnifying glass to be seen) can be neatened slightly when the paint goes on. The watercolour goes on last or the gold leaf will stick to that as well.

Sometimes a small painting is incorporated into the design. Henry does this separately on a little oval or round of Ivorine, usually no bigger than a fingernail. The Ivorine is cut to size and the edges are filed flat by rubbing the base over a piece of wet-and-dry sanding paper, so that it will sit properly on the surface. It gives an interesting effect by being slightly raised when it is inserted in the border design. The picture is stuck down with a rubberised solution or wood glue.

The finished work is framed to the client's choice. If a wooden moulding or a metal frame is used, Henry uses convex glass.

Detail showing Henry Saxon's amazing use of gold leaf. His illumination work takes us almost full circle back to the illuminated manuscript and the origin of miniatures.

A Hat Worn at the Balloon Race
watercolour on paper
by Marcelle Shears

Actual size

Silhouettes

Marcelle D. Shears

Watercolour on Paper, Vellum, Antique Ivory and Traditional Plaster

When Marcelle Shears does commissioned silhouettes from life, she has to be disciplined in her approach. Her first aim is to achieve an exact likeness. Once this is done: 'You have "set" the subject and it just takes itself assiduously through from beginning to end.' Her other work consists of the 'Costume' series, the 'Enchanted' series and the 'Carefree' series, for example silhouettes from nursery rhymes. The costumes involve extensive research in books and museums. She may portray just the head and bust but full-length figures show the whole costume to the best effect. The delightful fairies and nursery rhymes are probably her most relaxed work and she seems to have a lot of fun doing them. Although working in what is basically black and white, she endeavours to suggest colour by using all the different blacks. She also introduces fascinating detail and extra information.

She sometimes adds quite a lot of colour work to her silhouettes, which is allowable as long as the skin remains black. Silhouettes started as plain black 'shades' but colour was introduced in the eighteenth century. Marcelle likes the muted tones best. When she adds highlights to clothes and hair it is very delicately done. For her 'Costume' and other series, Marcelle makes three or four rough drawings to build up to her final composition. When she feels she has 'got it right', she draws directly on to the watercolour paper she is going to use, throwing away the roughs. She insists the paper must be acid free as she is very particular about conservation. For larger paintings she has to stretch the paper but for miniatures she prefers not to do so; it tends to slightly disturb and alter the hot pressed surface, which is detrimental to the crisp finish and would be a definite disadvantage for the detail she puts into her miniature work. If the silhouette is to be printed for commercial purposes she often uses Frisk (SC10), which is a good smooth surface paper.

She cuts a mask or mount fractionally bigger than the size of the finished picture so that if she does a wash

Paints
(usual palette)
Mainly Winsor & Newton artists' quality watercolours, in tubes. She has primaries and all the blacks:
Ivory Black
Jet Black
Lamp Black
Blue Black
Chinese white
Gouache (usually for larger areas than miniatures). She dates the tubes when she buys them.

Base
Arches Aquarelle or Sanders Waterford 90 lb hot-pressed watercolour paper.

Brushes
Winsor & Newton, series 12, sizes 000-2. She trims them when they become worn down.

Other materials
3H-4H pencils
Purified water (from a chemist's decanted into two small pots, one for washing the brush, the other for diluting the paint.
Kitchen paper
Gold and silver, in tablet form.
Magnifying glass

Andrea, by Marcelle Shears, shown actual size. Marcelle puts more variations in to black than most people would imagine possible. Her silhouettes are little masterpieces of detail.

Right
Enlargement showing Marcelle's control of fine lines.

to the edge it will be neat and covered when it is framed. Using a 3H or 4H pencil she draws the subject in very lightly: 'You could go up to a 6H but if you are the least bit heavy-handed you can make a line in the paper which marks it permanently and then you have had it!'

Once the drawing is done, she outlines everything with black paint: the flowers, the lace and the jewellery are all drawn in with a fine brush. Then she does the shadows — Ivory Black is her choice for this because it is softer, and if she wants to sharpen up the edges she uses Lamp Black to add emphasis. Then the larger areas of plain black are filled in. This can take a couple of washes one over the other. Each layer of wash should be allowed to dry between applications and finally left to harden, preferably overnight. Anybody trying black as a wash for the first time needs to practise. The paint has to be the right consistency and it has to be applied with confidence. Part of the art of silhouette painting is the even, velvety matt black — the edge must be completely crisp and accurate, and the blank black part completely uniform. The delicate hairs around the hairline are drawn in afterwards with a fine brush.

Highlights of gold, silver or colour often go on top of the black layers, when these are completely dry. Earrings and other jewellery require a light and deft touch; if the surface is touched too often there is a danger the paint will start to lift off. Marcelle uses genuine gold and silver in tablet form to which a little water is added, similar to using pans of watercolour paint. If white is required she uses Chinese White. The final 25 per cent of the work is mainly fine lines and is done under a magnifying glass to check the detail. She puts her initials on the front and signs the back of the finished work.

Most of Marcelle's frames are in the traditional style for miniatures. She includes individual labels for the back of her frames usually in Indian Ink — a design of flowers or something appropriate, as well as providing information on the work.

Miniature Painting Societies

United Kingdom

ROYAL SOCIETY OF MINIATURE PAINTERS, SCULPTORS AND GRAVERS
also
THE HILLIARD SOCIETY
Burwood House, 15 Union Street, Wells, Somerset BA5 2PU

SOCIETY OF LIMNERS
104 Poverest Road, Orpington, Kent BR5 2D

United States of America

MINIATURE ART SOCIETY OF FLORIDA
2401 Ecuadorian Way No.5, Clearwater, Florida 34623

MINIATURE ART SOCIETY OF GEORGIA
922 Blackwell Court, Marietta, Georgia 30066

MINIATURE ART SOCIETY OF MONTANA
2422 Brentwood Lane, Billings, Montana 59102

MINIATURE ARTISTS OF AMERICA
4829 Sunnybrook Drive, Newport Richey, Florida 34653

MINIATURE PAINTERS · SCULPTORS · GRAVERS SOCIETY OF WASHINGTON DC
1607 Crittendon Street, Washington DC 20011

Australia

AUSTRALIAN SOCIETY OF MINIATURE ART (ASMA):

ASMA New South Wales (Inc)
12 Ann Street, Willoughby, Sydney, New South Wales

ASMA Queensland (Inc)
PO Box 5358, Gold Coast Mail Centre, Bundall, Queensland 4217

ASMA Victoria (Inc)
PO Box 383, Eltham, Melbourne, Victoria 3095

ASMA Tasmania (Inc)
Hibiscus Gallery, 5 Ashfield Street, Sandy Bay, Hobart, Tasmania 7005

South Africa

SOUTH AFRICAN SOCIETY OF MINIATURE ART
PO Box 1450, Cramerview 2060, South Africa

Suppliers

United Kingdom

Fine art supplies

CORNELISSENS
105 Great Russell Street, London WC1B 3RY

Frames and materials

R J W PRODUCTS
1 Georgian Close, Hayes, Bromley Kent BR2 7RA

R S FRAMES
4 Broomfield Road, Sunbury-on-Thames, Middlesex TW16 6SW

POLYMERS PLUS
PO Box 101, Christchurch, Dorset BH23 7ES

Parchment and vellum

WILLIAM COWLEY
97 Caldecote Street, Newport Pagnell, Buckinghamshire MK16 ODB

Permanent selection of modern miniatures

LLEWELLYN ALEXANDER (FINE PAINTINGS) LTD
124-126 The Cut, Waterloo, London SE1 8LN